Shropshire

40 Heritage & History Walks

AF324376

The author and publisher have made every effort to ensure that the information in this publication is accurate, and accept no responsibility whatsoever for any loss, injury or inconvenience experienced by any person or persons whilst using this book.

published by
pocket mountains ltd
The Old Church, Annanside,
Moffat DG10 9HB

ISBN: 978-1-916739-04-8

Text and photography copyright © Derek Houghton 2025

The right of Derek Houghton to be identified as the Author of this work has been asserted by him in accordance with the Copyright, Designs and Patents Act 1988

A catalogue record for this book is available from the British Library

Contains Ordnance Survey data © Crown copyright and database 2025

All rights reserved. No part of this publication may be reproduced, stored in a retrieval system, or transmitted in any form or by any means, electronic or mechanical, including photocopying and recording, unless expressly permitted by Pocket Mountains Ltd.

Printed by J Thomson Colour Printers, Glasgow

Introduction

Shropshire has long been regarded as a hidden gem, often overlooked by those heading for the bigger challenges found in the rugged hills of Wales, and some way behind the popularity of the picturesque hotspots of England such as the Cotswolds or the Lake District.

Regular visitors will tell you, however, that there are few better places for curious walkers. As well as several well-established walking routes such as the Offa's Dyke Path and the Shropshire Way, there are countless waymarked paths that cover every part of the county. The Shropshire Hills Area of Outstanding Natural Beauty (AONB) is home to the 'blue remembered hills' of the original Shropshire Lad, A E Housman, and understandably attracts lots of visitors (see our companion guide, *The Welsh Marches: 40 Town and Country Walks*), yet there are many parts of the county – one of the most sparsely populated in England – where you will have the path to yourself.

The 40 walks in this volume are spread all around the region, taking in hills and dales which are home to Bronze Age stone circles, battle-scarred castles and fine country houses, and following the rivers and canals that brought pioneering engineers and ironmasters the raw materials needed to power the innovations which placed Shropshire – in particular, the Ironbridge Gorge on the River Severn – at the very centre of the Industrial Revolution.

History and heritage

It has been said that more has happened in the last 600 million years in Shropshire than anywhere of similar size in Britain, and arguably in the world. Originally located somewhere near the South Pole, the movement of tectonic plates and continental collisions moved the county slowly north, creating the coral reef which formed Wenlock Edge, the glacial tors of the Stiperstones, the fossil-rich desert sandstones of Grinshill and the rich coal seams laid down by decaying tropical rainforests, which were so fundamental to the industrial development of England. Around 150 million years ago, dinosaurs are likely to have roamed around Shropshire and, following the ice age, herds of mammoths certainly did; the bones of one adult and four juveniles were discovered near Shrewsbury in 1986.

The first Shropshire locals constructed stone circles and round barrows in the rolling hills, while the Celtic Cornovii tribe had their largest hillfort on top of The Wrekin overlooking the Roman legionary fortress at Wroxeter. In medieval times, the Mercian King Offa dug a massive earthwork to define the boundary between his lands and those of the Welsh.

In the 9th and 10th centuries, however, it was the equally unwelcome Danes who pillaged their way around the county and it wasn't long before the Normans arrived from France to impose a bit of law and order, establishing their tax-raising estates and hunting forests. Again, the Welsh kept the new lords busy and border skirmishing led to the building of a formidable double line of well-fortified castles; remarkably, of the nearly 200 castles in England, more than 30 are in Shropshire.

When not warring with the neighbours, the lords were fighting rebellious barons; the best-known bloody showdown was near Shrewsbury in 1403 between the armies of Henry IV and Henry 'Hotspur' Percy. When Civil War broke out in the 17th century, Shropshire (mostly) declared for the losing side and after the future King Charles II first failed to regain his father's throne he made his escape from Parliamentary forces disguised as a Shropshire farmhand, famously hiding in the branches of an oak tree. The only place in England which still happily celebrates Charles II's eventual return to the throne on Oak Apple Day (which was abolished everywhere else in 1859) is the little village of Aston on Clun in the Clun Valley.

It was the area's mineral riches and powerfully-flowing rivers which brought prosperity and people to Shropshire. The county is littered with reminders of early industry, from mills that prepared sheep fleeces for spinning to lead mines which, at their peak, produced almost half of the total output of the 'miracle metal' in England. Canals, and then railways, connected Shropshire with the world, and the iron ore which was smelted by Abraham Darby and others in the village

of Ironbridge on the River Severn was exported around the Empire. The cast-iron bridge which still spans the gorge is an enduring symbol of the change wrought by industry and in 1986 the gorge area was made a UNESCO World Heritage Site.

Shropshire remains, however, largely a rural county, rich in productive farmland with several historic market towns that have a long history of festivals and fair days, full of beautiful Tudor, Georgian and Victorian buildings, but no cities – the main urban hubs being the county town of Shrewsbury, one of England's finest medieval towns perfectly situated in a loop of the River Severn, and Telford, the most populous settlement, which was developed as a new town in the 1970s.

Don't be misled by the sleepy country air, however; many discoveries, ideas and innovations which have resonated around the world originated here. The first Parliament of English commoners and nobles was assembled in a tithe barn near Acton Burnell by Edward I, and the flame of the modern Olympic Games was lit by the visionary Dr William Penny Brookes in unassuming Much Wenlock. The county is also the birthplace of naturalist Charles Darwin, the childhood home of humorist and author P G Wodehouse (who called Shropshire the 'nearest earthly place to paradise'), and where the Scottish engineering genius Thomas Telford spent much of his illustrious career, building the county's roads, bridges and canals.

About this guide

The routes in this guide vary in length from an hour's stroll to a full morning or afternoon of walking. Most of the routes are circular and generally the walking is on well-used and maintained paths, lanes and tracks, with good waymarking, which should result in less time and energy spent on navigation.

The route descriptions found here cover the main points of navigation, but will not feature every detail along the route. Sketch maps are intended to be illustrative only and, for any more complex routes, it is recommended that you take the relevant OS map with you, as set out at the start of every walk.

Each walk is accompanied by a suggested walking time based on an average walking speed of 4kmph, with a small allowance added in on some hillier routes. While it goes without saying that everyone's pace is different, the seasons should also be a factor in how much time you allow for a walk. In spring and summer, progress can be hampered by signposts and smaller paths and stiles becoming swamped by nettles and fast-growing hedges, while after heavy rain crossing field sections, in particular, can become more of a slog.

Good-quality waterproof footwear should be worn on most of the walks and waterproofs are essential on some of the hillier walks, such as those up The Wrekin or on the Long Mynd, where the weather can often change rapidly.

In many parts of Shropshire, sheep, arable and dairy farming can all be encountered on the same walk. Dogs should be kept on a lead on farmland, and cattle just released from winter shelters or which have recently calved should be left well alone. If in doubt, it is usually possible to find a short detour to avoid such livestock.

Getting around

Shrewsbury and Telford are both easily accessible by train and there are 19 National Rail stations in Shropshire on various lines, including at Shrewsbury, Church Stretton, Ludlow, Telford Central, Wellington, Cosford and Whitchurch.

Bus timetables are available online at traveline.info. In summer months, the Shropshire Hills Shuttle Bus wends its way from Church Stretton around south Shropshire, usually stopping at Ratlinghope, Wentnor, Snailbeach, the Stiperstones National Nature Reserve and Carding Mill Valley. Information can be found at shropshirehills-nl.org.uk.

Car parking can be tricky in many small villages and hamlets. Some pubs may allow you to use their parking area if you intend to visit before or after your walk, but permission should be sought first. Walkers should always be sensitive to the needs and access of local residents when parking outwith public car parks.

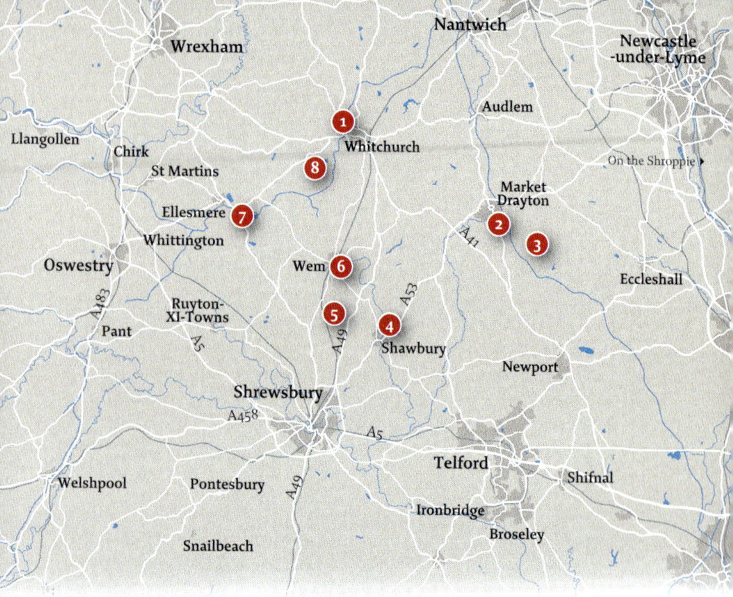

The meres and mosses of rural north Shropshire form part of the largest natural network of pools and wetlands outside of the Lake District in England. The main bog, a National Nature Reserve composed of Fenn's, Whixall and Bettisfield Mosses, lies between Ellesmere and Whitchurch. These 'Marches Mosses' are home to birds, insects, amphibians, reptiles and mammals, and a wide range of flora. In recent years, local conservation projects have reversed the damage of centuries of peat cutting.

Nearby are the placid meres of Ellesmere and Colemere, two of the nine lakes formed by retreating glaciers in the area which, unlike other lakes, are not fed by streams or rivers, but maintained by the water table and run-off from surrounding land.

Apart from the mosses and meres, there is no shortage of fertile farmland in the region and the four main market towns (Ellesmere, Wem, Market Drayton and Whitchurch) remain at the heart of the rural economy. The network of canals which transported farm produce from here to the rest of England and further afield are now popular with leisure cruisers, and restored stretches of the Llangollen, Ellesmere and 'Shroppie' canals provide some excellent walks.

Other circuits in this chapter visit an historic ruined mansion north of the village of Shawbury and the geological treasurehouse of Grinshill.

North Shropshire

Whitchurch and Grindley Brook Locks

Distance 10.3km **Time** 2 hours 30
Terrain roads, footpaths and canal path
Map OS Explorer 257 **Access** trains to
Whitchurch from Shrewsbury and Crewe;
regular buses from Shrewsbury

**Whitchurch is a characterful market town
in the north of Shropshire full of half-
timbered buildings and independent
shops, as well as its own branch of
Thomas Telford's Llangollen Canal.
This route circles the town to meet the
canal at the village of Grindley Brook,
home to the steepest series of locks on
the waterway, before returning to town.**

Start from Whitchurch railway station
and head along Station Road towards the
town centre. Go right at the traffic lights
onto Brownlow Street and right along
Claypit Street soon after. Keep straight on
along Alport Road, passing the entrance
to the Community Hospital, and take a
left on quiet Terrick Road.

Once past the golf course, look out for a
left turn onto a 'green lane' section of the
Bishop Bennet Way, a 55km-long route
which runs from Beeston Castle to nearby
Wirswall. Popular with horse-riders and
mountain-bikers, as well as walkers, the
route is named after an 18th-century
clergyman and member of the House of
Lords who pioneered the study of
England's Roman roads.

Follow this path to join a farm track
which emerges on the A49. Take care
crossing the road and continue to follow
the signposted bridleway and access road
for Hinton Manor. After Hinton Bank
Farm, follow the path as it turns left onto
another bridleway which passes through
the fields of Grindley Brook Farm on the
way to meet the Llangollen Canal.

Once at the canal, turn left for the
Grindley Brook Locks, a series of six locks,
three of which make a staircase with a
total rise of almost six metres. Well

looked-after by the Canal & River Trust and the local community, volunteer lock-keepers help around 6000 boats make their way through here every year.

The village is also the starting point for four long-distance footpaths; the Maelor, Shropshire and South Cheshire Ways and the Sandstone Trail, and several others run through here, including the Marches Way.

To return to Whitchurch, simply follow the delightful curving path alongside the busy canal and pass under the A41 to arrive at a drawbridge. Follow the branch of the canal here, known as the Arm, which allows touring canal-users to berth their boats and visit the town centre. In its heyday, the canal reached further into town where there was a wharf area and canal-side corn and silk mills. This short section was re-opened in 1993 following great effort by locals to bring canal traffic back to Whitchurch.

Shropshire Way signposts lead back through the Waterway Park and round to Victoria Jubilee Park; at the end of the park turn left for the town centre and the railway station.

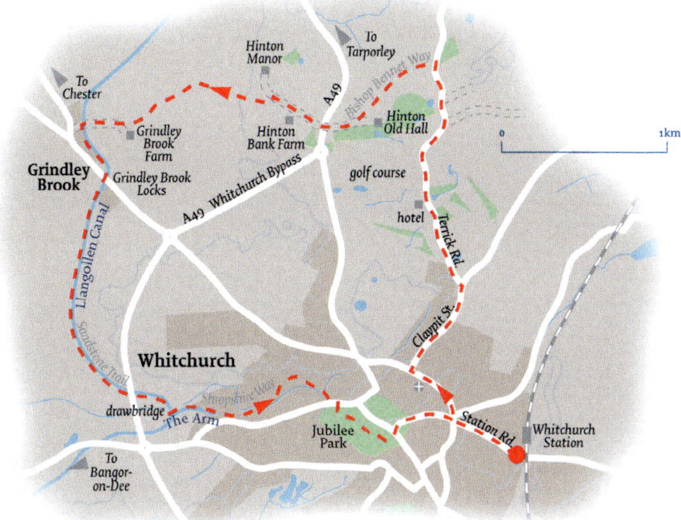

Market Drayton and Tyrley Locks

Distance 11km **Time** 2 hours 45
Terrain canal paths, county lanes, field
and woodland paths **Map** OS Explorer 243
Access regular buses to Market Drayton
from Shrewsbury

First granted a charter for a weekly
Wednesday market in 1245 by Henry III,
bustling Market Drayton is often seen as
the quintessential Shropshire market
town. Famed for its Buttercross market
shelter and the spicy gingerbread baked
here for centuries from recipes brought
back from the Crusades, it has a rich
commercial history. This walk takes in a
peaceful section of the Shroppie (the
Shropshire Union Canal) before returning
to town via the surrounding countryside.

Start from the Swimming and Fitness
Centre on the edge of town off Newport
Road (A529). Exit the car park and turn left
to join Phoenix Bank heading towards the
town centre with a view of St Mary's
Church up on the left.

At the junction, turn right into Great
Hales Street and follow it to meet Stafford
Street. Turn right here and continue onto
Newcastle Road, then bear left at Betton
Road to reach the bridge over the
Shropshire Union Canal.

Go down to the canal path and pass
under the bridge, heading for Tyrley
Locks. Completed in 1835 to link the West
Midlands and Liverpool, the Shroppie
remains an important waterway,
attracting thousands of boaters every
year, and there are usually several boats
parked up at the moorings here.

Follow the canal over the Berrisford
Aqueduct and on through a stretch of
peaceful countryside to reach the first of
the five Tyrley Locks. As the first lock, the
bottom lock, comes into view the canal
appears to have been cut out of the rock at

each side which gives an impressive insight into the work required to construct the canal. The last of the locks is reached at Tyrley Wharf by a bridge and buildings which were once canal workers' cottages and stables.

Leave the canal by the Tyrley Road, heading towards the A529; after crossing this road, which can be busy, go straight onto Sandy Lane by the side of the roadside inn. Carry on along the lane until it turns sharply right to return to town; to continue on the full circuit, however, go left, following the rough signposted track.

The track skirts the golf course to emerge by the clubhouse on Sutton Lane.

Turn left and look for a metal gate into the fields on the other side of the road. Follow the path from here to reach some farm buildings.

Keep right around the field edge (ignoring the stile) to pass the private road to Buntingsdale Hall. Carry straight on to Buntingsdale Road and shortly after crossing a bridge over the River Tern, continue to Bottom Lane, a signposted gravel track leading off the road on the right. Follow this to the end, then bear left up a small incline to reach Tern View. Turn right onto Quarry Bank Road at the end, keeping to this road as it eventually becomes Walkmill Road to return to the start.

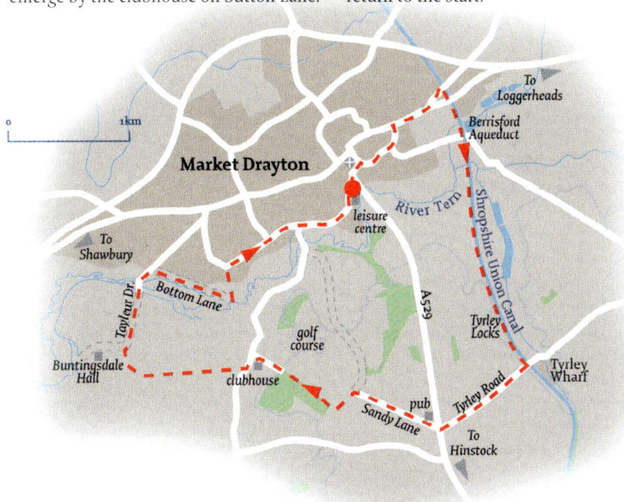

Cheswardine and Goldstone Wharf

Distance 7km **Time** 2 hours
Terrain footpaths, fields and pavement;
several stiles **Map** OS Explorer 243
Access no public transport to the start

The peaceful rural village of Cheswardine is located south of Market Drayton and a stone's throw from the Shropshire Union Canal. A break at the popular canalside inn by Goldstone Wharf is recommended after the initial tour of country lanes, fields and woodland north of the village.

The walk starts from the parish hall and community shop (parking available) on Podmore Road, just off the High Street. From here, make your way towards St Swithun's Church which looks over the village from the top of the High Street.

Carry on past the church along Lawn Lane. To the right, behind the trees, is the moat, buried ruins and earthworks of long-gone Cheswardine Castle, said to have once been owned by Lady Godiva, wife of the powerful Earl Leofric, who famously protested against her husband's harsh tax demands by riding her horse naked through the streets of Coventry.

Stay on Lawn Lane as the track becomes a path and after a few hundred metres bear left through a field as it forks. This leads to a stile and bridge at the edge of the hazel woodland of Lawn Drumble. Continue to go over a second stile and keep to the field edge to reach another woodland, Haywood Drumble. Make your way through the trees and out again to follow another field edge. At a marker post make a sharp left turn to cross the field and go through the woodland again.

From here, follow the field edges to reach a farm track beyond the trees by

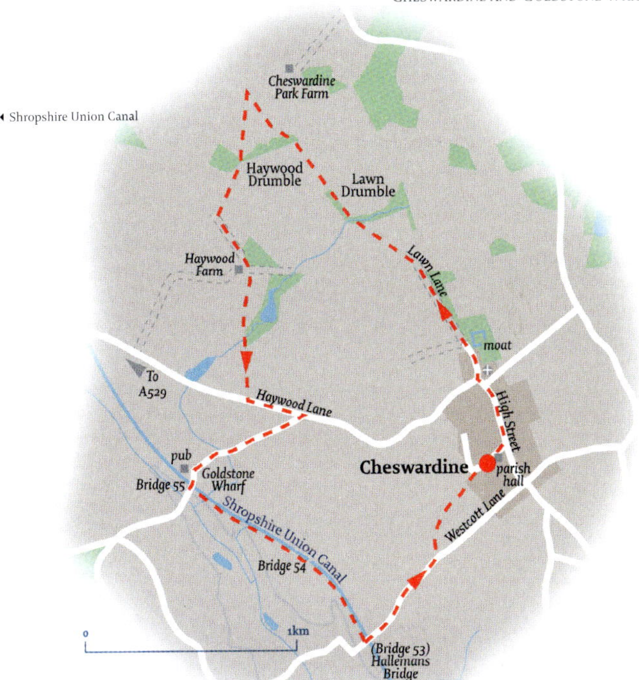

Haywood Farm. Go along this to pass the farm buildings and continue across a field and down into woodland. Go through the trees and cut across the field to reach Haywood Lane. Look out for traffic as you go left along the road to reach the lane which leads down to the canalside Wharf Tavern and a caravan park. As well as a beer garden and moorings, there's a winding hole here which allows boaters to turn around.

Once at the Shroppie, cross Bridge No 55 (Goldstone Bridge) and take the path along the waterway to pass Bridge No 54. At Bridge No 53 (Hallemans Bridge), leave the canal and follow Wescott Lane back over the water to Cheswardine, being aware of traffic as you go.

You can miss out some road walking by looking out for a path off to the left which cuts across a field. Follow this along the hedge to a narrow lane which soon leads between houses to Podmore Road and the parish hall.

Moreton Corbet Castle

Distance 5.5km **Time** 1 hour 30
Terrain country roads, footpaths
Map OS Explorer 241 **Access** no public
transport to the start

**The beguiling battle-scarred ruins of
Moreton Corbet are the starting point for
this walk along quiet country lanes and
the route of the old Shropshire Way.**

The castle in Moreton Corbet started
out as an earth and timber stronghold for
a Saxon family around 1100 before being
replaced by stone 100 years later. In the
1560s Sir Andrew Corbet began to remodel
the castle into a spectacular Elizabethan
mansion and his son Robert carried on
the work.

During the English Civil Wars, Sir
Vincent Corbet fought for the king and
the castle became a base for Shrewsbury's
Royalist soldiers. Although besieged
several times by Parliamentarian forces, it
survived the skirmishing with just a few
marks from musket shot which are still
visible on the mansion's east and south
sandstone walls. The Corbet family
eventually lost interest in the house and
it was left to become the romantic ruin
you see today.

Start the walk from the parking area in
front of the castle ruins. After exploring
the English Heritage site (free entry),
make your way to St Bartholomew's
Church. Among other interesting features
inside are several Corbet family funerary
monuments, including two unusual
richly-detailed and painted chest tombs,
and a dazzling altar canopy.

From the church continue to the junction at the end of the road. Turn right for Stanton upon Hine Heath and follow the road over the River Roden, then turn right towards St Andrew's Church when you reach the village.

After visiting the church and churchyard, double back and go down Church Lane to pick up the old Shropshire Way. Follow this trail through a couple of gates and across fields alongside a woodland. Cross a bridge over a small stream and follow the edge of the field towards Sowbath Farm. Keep to the marked path around the property which leads along the farm's driveway to soon emerge on the busy Shrewsbury to Market Drayton road.

Turn right and walk 100m along the roadside to the end of the quiet country road which will take you back to Moreton Corbet. There are good views of the castle from the road and throughout the walk there are likely to be helicopters flying low from RAF Shawbury, the nearby training centre for pilots which was attended by both Prince William and Prince Harry.

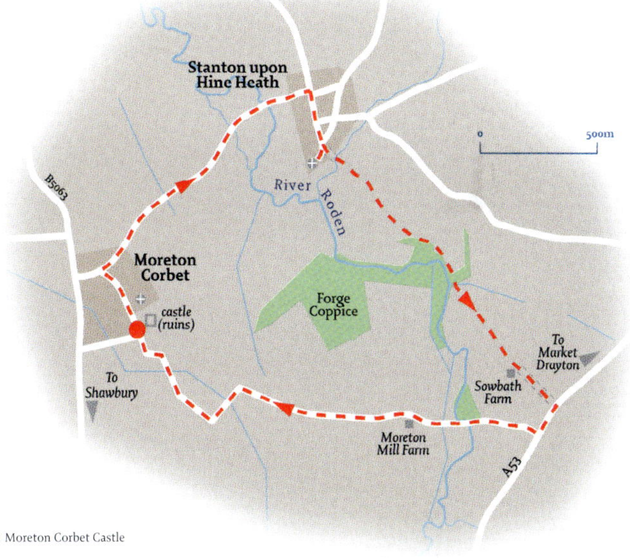

Grinshill and Corbet Wood

Distance 5km **Time** 1 hour 30
Terrain country roads and woodland
paths; steep ascent and descent
Map OS Explorer 241 **Access** regular buses
to Yorton from Shrewsbury; regular trains
from Shrewsbury and Crewe

**The summit viewpoint on the sandstone
Grinshill ridge has fantastic views over
the Shropshire Hills, the Welsh border
and Shrewsbury. This circuit takes in the
192m-high hill and adjacent Corbet Wood
Local Nature Reserve, starting from the
railway station in Yorton and returning
via the village of Grinshill.**

From the station in Yorton, go under
the bridge (if arriving from Shrewsbury),
pass the former Railway Inn and walk up
the narrow road to Clive. Once in the
village, continue along the High Street
to Drawwell with the All Saints Church
at the top of the road.

After going up Drawwell, take the path
uphill to the left of the church lychgate
which leads to the local primary school.
Just past the school, you'll find a
woodland path off to the right which
takes you to the viewpoint on Grinshill.

Views across Shrewsbury begin to open
up as you make your way to the summit
which provides a splendid panorama,
taking in The Wrekin round Wenlock
Edge, Caer Caradoc and The Lawley,
Breidden Hill and the Berwyns. Be aware
that the edge of the rocky outcrop has a
severe drop, so care is needed.

The walk out from the top requires
a slight backtrack to the path, then

continue on, bearing right along the wooded path into Corbet Wood Local Nature Reserve. The conifer and broad-leaved trees here provide an ideal habitat for birds, including coal tits, warblers, woodpeckers, and goldcrests. More than 120 species of butterfly and moth have also been recorded on the site. The wood is designated as a Site of Special Scientific Interest (SSSI) for its geological importance. Look carefully and you might see fossilised sand dunes, rain prints and differing layers of rock formations; there are plenty of other paths to explore.

Keep an eye out too for signs of industry around the site; copper mining once took place here, as well as quarrying; Lord Hill's Column in Shrewsbury is made from Grinshill stone, as are the English and Welsh Bridges in Shrewsbury, some local churches and the lintel of the door of Number 10 Downing Street.

Quite steep descents require care when wet before the path joins a track (Sandy Lane) at the rear of the village hall. Turning right here will take you along the signposted Shropshire Way into Grinshill. Pass All Saints Church before reaching the road for Yorton and turning right.

This section of road is quieter than the earlier section to Clive, although care needs to be taken as you return to Yorton Station, passing Hope Farm and the entrance to Sansaw Hall on the way.

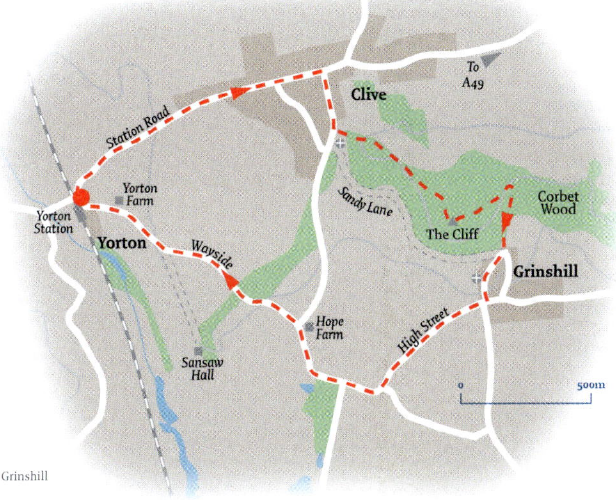

Wem and Tilley

Distance 7.5km **Time** 2 hours
Terrain pavements and footpaths; some
road sections **Map** OS Explorer 241
Access regular buses and trains to Wem
from Shrewsbury

The market town of Wem is a mecca
for sweet pea enthusiasts. Developed by
Henry Eckford, a Scottish horticulturist
who settled here in 1888, his Grandiflora
sweet pea variety is now grown around
the world and his contribution to
gardening is celebrated at Wem's Sweet
Pea Show, which, along with the annual
carnival, brings a riot of colour to the
town every summer. This rural circuit
visits the nearby village of Tilley before
returning to Wem by the River Roden.

From Wem Station, make your way over
the level crossing when safe to do so and
bear right onto Aston Road.

Continue on the pavement past
Orchard Way and soon after, go right on
a signposted track which leads to a
footpath. This is part of the
old Shropshire Way and continues to a
metal footbridge over the River Roden.
Cross over and continue on the footpath
to the end of Weir Lane, then follow the
lane between hedgerows to the road at
Barkers Green.

Turn right and follow the quiet road
past fields and houses to the busier
Shawbury Road. Go straight over this and
continue on the road for Tilley until you
reach the Shropshire Way which crosses
the road in front of you.

Enter the field to your right here and go
between ponds to follow the line of
telegraph poles across the field. Once
through the field gate, continue on the
farm access road to the main Shrewsbury

◀ The River Roden and Wem Mill's chimney

Road. Cross straight over, go through a metal gate and take the often overgrown winding path towards the railway line where there is a pedestrian crossing which leads into Tilley.

Tilley is notable for the number of medieval and post-medieval timber buildings in the village. Between 2014 and 2018 locals undertook a major dendrochronology (tree-ring dating) project centred on 19 of these historic buildings and the results were published in a book, *The Tilley Timber Project*.

On the other side of the village is a narrow path off to the right which leads to the River Roden. Cross the footbridge and follow the riverside path back to Mill Street in Wem. As you approach the town, you'll see the chimney of the old Wem Mill, a reminder that there were once six working watermills on this quiet river and its tributaries.

Back in Wem, follow Mill Street to St Peter and St Paul Church and the junction with the busy High Street. Turn right here to return to the station.

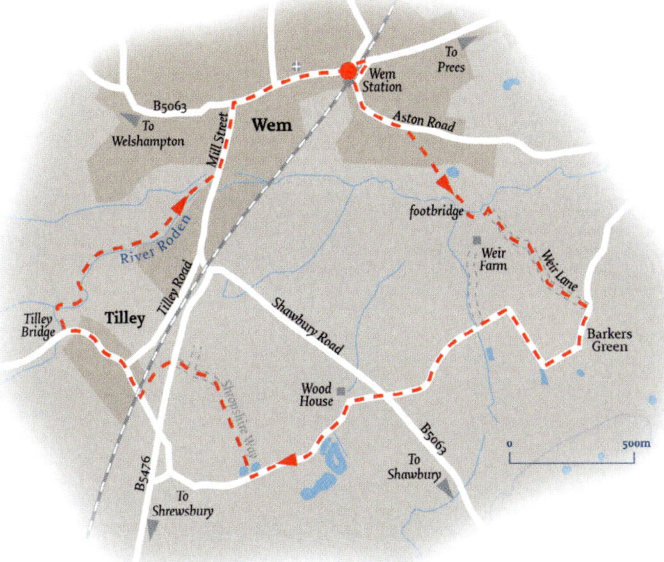

Ellesmere and Colemere

Distance 10.4km **Time** 2 hours 35
Terrain pavements, canal paths, quiet
roads, field and woodland paths
Map OS Explorer 241 **Access** regular buses
to Ellesmere from Shrewsbury

**Surrounded by mature woodland and
home to a variety of wildfowl and wading
birds, Colemere (or sometimes Cole Mere)
is one of Shropshire's most beautiful
meres, and the only one you can walk all
the way around. This route starts and
finishes in the busy market town of
Ellesmere, home to The Mere, one of the
largest natural meres in England outside
of the Lake District.**

Ellesmere attracts many people to walk,
boat, fish and relax by The Mere, one of
nine shallow lakes in the area – the others
are Blakemere, Crosemere, Kettlemere,

Newtonmere, Whitemere, Sweatmere,
Hanmer Mere and Colemere. The town
lies on the Llangollen Canal and there is a
wharf on a side arm of the canal near the
town centre. The construction of the canal
(originally called the Ellesmere Canal)
was overseen by Thomas Telford,
Shropshire's county surveyor. Originally
intended to connect the ironworks and
collieries of northeast Wales and the
manufacturing centres of the west
Midlands to the port of Liverpool (via
Ellesmere Port on the River Mersey), it
was never completed as planned due to
rising costs and the failure to attract
commercial traffic.

From the town centre, head towards
The Mere and follow the promenade east
past the kiosk café and The Boathouse,
then follow the path alongside the A495
as it leaves town. Cross over the road just
before the junction with the A528 to

Shrewsbury and go down the short path to the Llangollen Canal.

Turn left and immediately enter the 80m-long brick-lined Ellesmere Tunnel to Blakemere. Once through the tunnel, keep to the canal towpath for about 2km, passing Blakemere on the left, to arrive at Bridge No 55. Leave the canal path here and cross over the bridge, then walk down the road for a short distance past a thatched cottage, looking out for a gate for Colemere soon after.

Go through the gate and follow the mostly level woodland path (with a short section of boardwalk) around the mere in an anticlockwise direction, passing the sailing club at the far end. Rich in birdlife in all seasons, look out for snipe, curlew, goldeneye and pochard, as well as dragonflies and damselflies in summer, as you make your way around this peaceful Site of Special Scientific Interest (SSSI).

Once back at Bridge No 55, retrace your steps towards Blakemere and the Ellesmere Tunnel. After going through the tunnel, follow the canal all the way back into Ellesmere, passing the marina at Blackwater Meadow just before the junction with the Ellesmere arm of the canal. Across the water you can see Beech House, the old headquarters of the Ellesmere Canal Company.

Cross the last bridge and continue to the end of the canal arm at Ellesmere Wharf with its restored goods yard crane and surviving brick warehouse. Bear right along Wharf Road and onto Scotland Street to return to the town centre.

◄ Ellesmere Wharf

The Marches Mosses

Distance 7.5km **Time** 2 hours
Terrain footpath and canal towpath
Map OS Explorer 241 **Access** no public
transport to the start

Fenn's, Whixall and Bettisfield Mosses
– collectively known as 'The Marches
Mosses' – are peatlands which were
drained and damaged by commercial peat
cutting before being designated as a
National Nature Reserve (NNR) in 1991
and set on the road to recovery. Keep your
eyes peeled for otters along the canal
section and the rare long-legged raft
spider around the ponds.

The entrance to the mosses is located
south of Whitchurch by the border with
Wales, not far from Whixall Marina on the
Prees Branch of the Ellesmere Canal. The
visitor car park is found at the end of
Moss Lane on the other side of a
drawbridge over the Llangollen Canal.

From the car park, take the path along
the canal, following the signs for the
Mammoth Tower. This section of the
Llangollen Canal is soon joined by the
Prees Branch of the Ellesmere Canal just
after the Roving Bridge. This unusual
design allowed horses to transfer canal
sides without being unhitched from their
boats. A few hundred metres on you
arrive at the viewing tower.

Opened in 2020 and standing 5m high,
this tower offers a fantastic view of the
Fenn's and Whixall Mosses and is
surrounded by information boards.
Apparently the peat depth 150 years ago
was the height of the tower which
highlights the damage caused by peat
extraction and drainage.

From the tower, return to the canal and
continue along to the border with Wales.
After a few hundred metres, turn right to
enter Fenn's Moss. The paths around the

mosses can be damp, uneven and soggy, so care is required to stay on the path and not to wander onto deep, flooded and partially vegetated ditches.

This area was used as a Royal Field Artillery School during the First World War and as a bombing range in the Second World War. It was also a decoy site to divert night bombers from their intended targets. If you look up today, you have a chance of seeing common buzzard, kestrel, peregrine, sparrowhawk and short-eared owls here. The acrobatic and agile little hobby falcon is an especially good sighting; look out for them dashing around and swooping

down to catch dragonflies. Keep your eyes open for adders – Britain's only poisonous snake – on the moss as well.

The paths are well-marked and, after a short distance, there is a right turn and in a few hundred metres, a left turn towards some ponds and information boards. Continue straight before making a right turn to meet up with a section of the waymarked Shropshire Way.

Continue on the Shropshire Way as you turn right at a wooded area with a field on the left and follow this for a few hundred metres before turning left to return to the car park, passing some old peat mill machinery on the way.

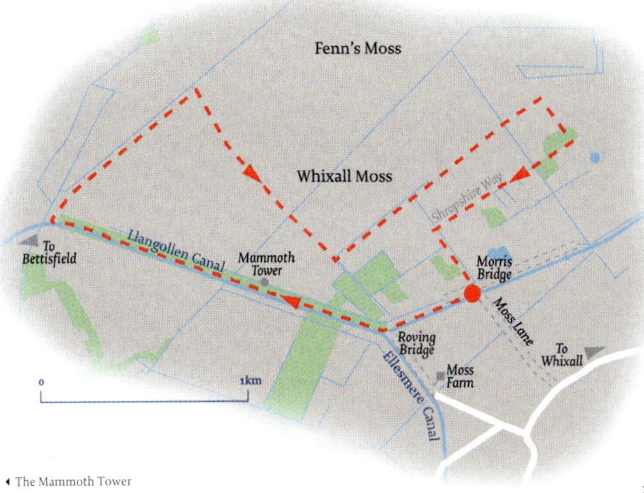

The English romance novelist and poet Mary Webb (1881-1927) described her home in south Shropshire as lying 'between the dimpled lands of England and the gaunt purple steeps of Wales, half in Faery and half out of it'.

This beguiling region remains a place that never fails to stir the imagination and the lively towns of Bishop's Castle, Craven Arms, Ludlow and Clun with their characteristic black-and-white Tudor buildings, make excellent bases from which to explore the area's patchwork of quiet valleys, rolling hills, ancient woodlands and heather moorland. The 'Little Switzerland' of Church Stretton, however, is the most popular with walkers. Surrounded by fine hills, the town sits at the foot of the Long Mynd, a vast heather-covered upland plateau cut with steep-sided valleys. Although many of the better-known paths can get busy at weekends and during the summer months, it is not hard to escape the crowds to explore the varied geology and diverse wildlife found here.

Being close to the border with Wales means that there are also several castle ruins to explore and the remarkable ancient earthwork of Offa's Dyke can be followed from the border town of Knighton, home to the Offa's Dyke Centre.

South Shropshire

Carding Mill Valley and the Long Mynd

Distance 9.5km **Time** 3 hours
Terrain footpath, rough path in places;
some scrambling **Map** OS Explorer 217
Access regular trains and buses to Church
Stretton from Shrewsbury

Known in Victorian times as 'Little
Switzerland', Church Stretton was where
the well-to-do came to escape the smoke
and grime of industrial England. Carding
Mill Valley, the site of an old woollen mill
on its western edge, is a popular access
point for the hills and waterfalls around
the former spa town and for exploring the
Long Mynd heath and moorland plateau.

Managed by the National Trust, Carding
Mill Valley's car park (no charge for NT
members) fills up quickly on weekends
and holidays with coach parties; arrive
early or use alternative parking in the
town – it's not far from the station if you
are arriving by train.

From the National Trust's Chalet
Pavilion tearoom and visitor centre,
escape the crowds and head for the hills
following the signs for the Lightspout
Waterfall. Once past the scattered houses,
there is a short detour to a sheltered
reservoir with a steep stone beach
surrounded by trees, which is popular
with cold water swimmers.

Once dried off, head back to the main
path and continue up the valley on Mott's
Road to a Y-junction. This old bridleway

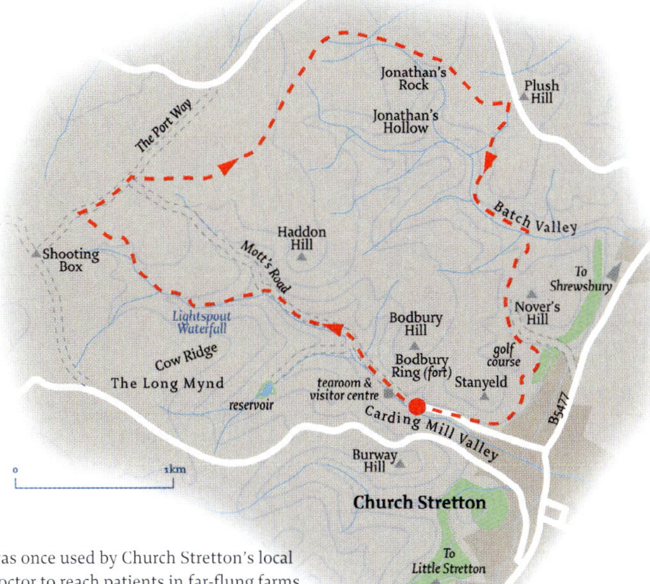

was once used by Church Stretton's local doctor to reach patients in far-flung farms.

Go left at the junction for the waterfall, following the stream on a path that is rocky and slippery when wet and requires a bit of careful scrambling in places. The 4m-high cascading waterfall – which Victorian visitors called a 'miniature Niagara' – is soon reached and the path continues steeply up rough stone steps to the right. At the top carry on gently climbing towards the Port Way on the Long Mynd rather than looping back around to Mott's Road and the main tearoom and car park.

Once on the Port Way there is an option to go left towards Shooting Box (487m) and continue on to Pole Bank (516m) which is the highest point on the Long Mynd. Turning right, however, soon takes you to a junction with Mott's Road and a grassy track which leads around to Plush Hill, passing the rocky outcrop of Jonathan's Rock on the way.

From Plush Hill, descend quite steeply into Batch Valley. Once in the valley go right through a gate and onto a rougher path with Nover's Hill to the left. Follow the path, enjoying views towards Caer Caradoc, The Lawley and The Wrekin in the distance before crossing a couple of holes on the golf course and returning to Carding Mill Valley and the car park.

◀ Lightspout Waterfall

Cleobury Mortimer round

Distance 9.2km **Time** 2 hours 30
Terrain footpath, country road and
bridleway **Map** OS Explorer 203
Access regular buses to Cleobury
Mortimer from Ludlow and Kidderminster

**The market town of Cleobury Mortimer
was the home of the postman writer
Simon Evans (1895-1940) who came to the
area to relieve respiratory injuries he
sustained when gassed during the First
World War. His daily round followed the
Rea Valley to Stottesdon and back and
inspired many radio broadcasts and five
popular books about rural Shropshire
between the wars. This walk takes in part
of the 25km walk named in his memory.**

Cleobury Mortimer lies midway
between Ludlow and Kidderminster, and
the car park is signposted on Childe Road
off the A4117 which runs through the
centre of town. Take the footpath from
the car park that leads to Love Lane and
go left to pass the Lacon Childe School.
Keep on the lane as it bears right, then go
left at the junction with Langland Road to
pass the town's primary school.

Carry on along a footpath and go
around the edge of the field to cross a
brook, then continue to pick up a farm
track heading north on the west side of
the River Rea. This is a section of the
160km-long Jack Mytton Way, which starts
in Cleobury Mortimer and allows
horseriders, cyclists and walkers to
explore some of Shropshire most unspoilt
countryside. The route is named after an
eccentric Regency landowner and
huntsman known locally as 'Mad Jack'.
He is said to have kept 2000 dogs for his
hunts, with his favourites fed on steak
and champagne, and served as an MP for

◀ St Mary's Church, Neen Savage

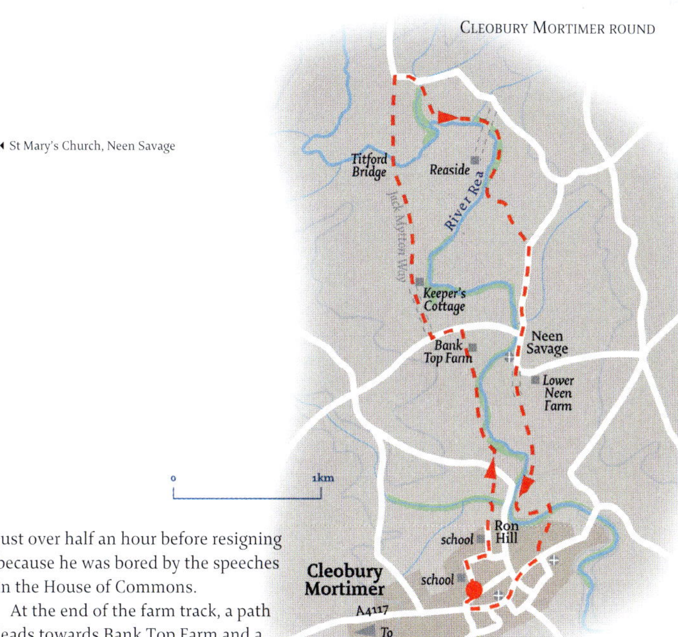

just over half an hour before resigning because he was bored by the speeches in the House of Commons.

At the end of the farm track, a path leads towards Bank Top Farm and a road. Go left at the road, then shortly after make a right turn onto another farm track and follow this straight for about 2km, crossing the river at Titford Bridge before reaching another road.

Turn right and follow the twisting lane to meet a section of the Simon Evans Way which keeps close to the River Rea. This can get rough and boggy in places but there are fine views towards Titterstone Clee Hill (533m) with its distinctive 'golf ball' radar station, and the Brown Clee Hills and Abdon Burf (540m) as the path makes its way to the road north of Neen Savage.

Just before the hamlet there is a ford over the Rea at the junction with the road to Bank Top Farm. Don't cross; instead carry on to the picturesque St Mary's Church, then bear right onto a farm track. This leads back to Cleobury Mortimer, either by the first bridge onto Ronhill Lane or further round the bend, via the bridge and footpath to Rockley Bank.

Either way, returning to the car park, look out for the unusual twisted shingle spire of the parish church which inspired the title of Evans' first collection of articles: *Round About the Crooked Steeple.*

Mortimer Forest

Distance 6.4km **Time** 2 hours
Terrain forest paths and roads
Map OS Explorer 203 **Access** no public
transport to the start

Straddling the Herefordshire and
Shropshire border, Mortimer Forest
covers the hilly ground just south of
Ludlow, which Sir John Betjeman
famously described as 'probably the
loveliest town in England'. There are
several access points, three car parks and
a number of waymarked trails; this route
leads to the summit of High Vinnalls
(375m) for a panoramic view of the area.

Originally made up of ancient royal
chases and deer parks, the forest derives
its name from the powerful Mortimer
dynasty, Norman lords who had a hand in
everything that happened in this area
during the Middle Ages when there was
frequent conflict between England and
Wales. The forest provided the Mortimer
stronghold of Ludlow Castle with wood
and other produce.

Managed by Forestry England today, the
1000-acre forest of larch, spruce and
Douglas fir replaced oak and other native
woodland in the 1920s when commercial
timber production was the priority. The
benefits of broadleaf trees in preserving
biodiversity are better understood now
and the forest is being gradually
replanted with native species.

The woodland is rich in wildlife; look
out for skylarks and red kite, and the
'long-haired' fallow deer only found in
this forest. Introduced by the Mortimer

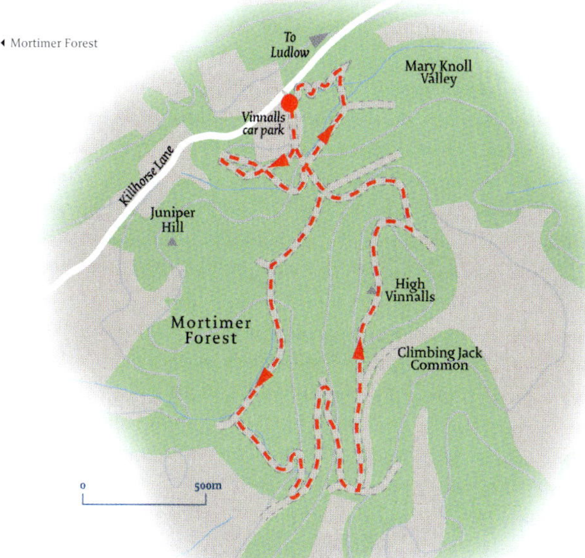

lords, these rare creatures have a hairier, curlier coat than the usual fallow deer.

From the Vinnalls car park off the Ludlow to Wigmore road (Killhorse Lane), southwest of Ludlow, follow the waymarked Vinnalls Loop on a level footpath before taking the forest road. Continue as it twists and turns up and down until it reaches the Mortimer Trail, a 48km long-distance linear footpath which connects Ludlow and Kington. Follow this above the treeline to the top of High Vinnalls.

Titterstone Clee and Brown Clee in Shropshire can be seen to the north, with the south Shropshire hills to the west, the Malvern Hills to the southeast and Bannau Brycheiniog (Brecon Beacons) in the southwest. On the eastern lower slope of High Vinnalls, the ditches of a Bronze Age fort are still visible.

From the top, continue down through the trees and rejoin the forest road followed earlier. Continue straight back to the car park or extend the walk with a short loop around a level trail. There is also an option to follow another track to explore the pleasant Mary Knoll Valley.

Craven Arms to Flounders' Folly

Distance 11.6km **Time** 4 hours 30 **Terrain** footpaths, fields and country roads **Map** OS Explorer 217 **Access** regular buses and trains to Craven Arms from Shrewsbury

The market town of Craven Arms is home to the excellent turf-roofed Shropshire Hills Discovery Centre which features exhibits about the county's geology, biology and history. This challenging walk starts from there and takes in Flounders' Folly, a 24m-high landmark tower on Callow Hill to the northeast of the town, built to mark the boundary between four large estates in 1838.

The Shropshire Hills Discovery Centre is located off Ludlow Road at the southern end of town. Pass through the mammoth tusk gateway behind the centre – a complete mammoth skeleton

was found in a quarry near Shrewsbury. This leads into Onny Meadows where you take the first left past some houses to cross the River Onny by a footbridge.

Follow the path bearing right across the field and continue through a gate and along the edge of the next field to reach the B4368 road. Cross over and continue up through Halford Wood to a marker post on the summit plateau. Go left here and soon Flounders' Folly will come into view on Callow Hill before you meet a road where you turn right for the hamlet of Lower Dinchope. Keep straight on past farm buildings to reach a signpost for Flounders' Folly next to a field gate. Go through the gate, paying attention to any livestock in the field, and bear right to reach the woodland, then turn left to

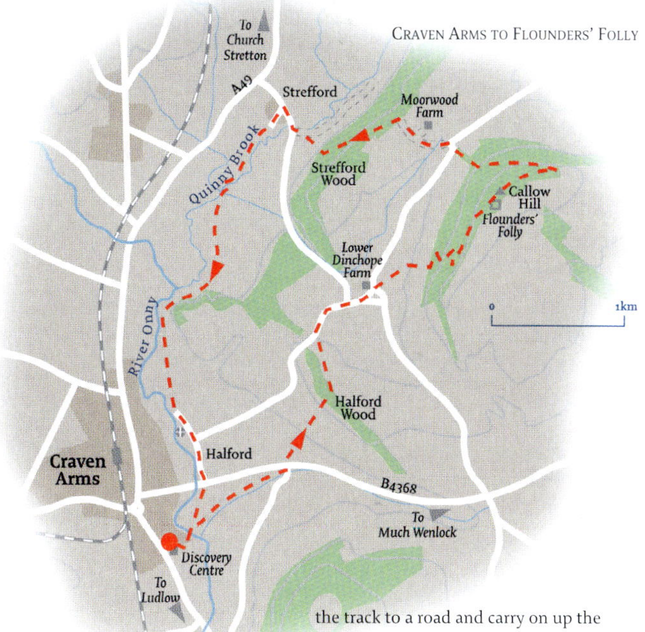

follow the path which zigzags steeply uphill through the trees. Once at the top, turn left along the path to arrive at Flounders' Folly on the exposed summit.

Named after Benjamin Flounders, the owner of the local Culmington Estate, the tower fell into disrepair in the 20th century before being restored in 2004-5 by the Flounders' Folly Trust. If the Cross of St George flag is flying from the flagpole then it is open to the public (usually one day a month), giving visitors the chance to climb the 78 stairs to enjoy the viewing platform.

From the tower, continue past the summit of the hill and soon dogleg down the track to a road and carry on up the access road to Moorwood Farm. Before the turn for the farm itself, bear left and continue through Strefford Wood. Leave the woods by a track which meets the road at Quinny Brook. Cross the footbridge by the side of the ford to enter the hamlet of Strefford.

Go left at the crossroads in Strefford and continue on a path which shadows the Quinny Brook to meet the River Onny. Keep on the path all the way to the hamlet of Halford on the outskirts of Craven Arms and pass St Thomas' Church shortly before arriving back at the B4368. Turn right and take the path before the bridge to return across the field to Onny Meadows and the Discovery Centre.

◄ Flounders' Folly and Callow Hill

Hopton Castle and Woods

Distance 6.75km **Time** 2 hours 30
Terrain footpaths and forest tracks
(some shared with mountain bikers)
Map OS Explorer 201 **Access** regular buses
to Hopton Heath (1.6km from the start)
from Ludlow; regular trains to Hopton
Heath from Shrewsbury

Set in a small valley halfway between
Knighton and Craven Arms, the village
of Hopton Castle takes its name from
the formidable castle here which was
bombarded and undermined in a month-
long siege during the English Civil War.
This walk starts from the romantic ruin
and explores the nearby woodland, a
popular destination for downhill
mountain biking, taking in the summit
and viewpoint of Hopton Titterhill.

At the time of the Civil War, Hopton
Castle was owned by the Wallop family,
isolated but steadfast Parliamentarians in
a predominantly Royalist county, and in
1644 a small garrison of 30 or so men was
besieged for a month before surrendering.
There are various accounts of what
happened next, but the end result is clear;
all those captured (apart from the
commander) were promptly executed and
unceremoniously thrown in a ditch.
Although the castle was rebuilt as a
fortified tower house, by the 18th century
it had been abandoned and it was only
the heroic efforts of a group of local
volunteers which saved this significant
ruin from further degradation.

From the castle, head out of the car park
into the village and go left along a stretch
of the Heart of Wales Line long-distance
trail past St Edward's Church.

A relatively unusual name for a church,
St Edward is regarded as the patron saint

◀ The ruin of Hopton Castle

of kings, difficult marriages and separated spouses. Continue past a footpath sign and stile (this is used on the return) to meet a farm gate with Heart of Wales Line signage.

Go through the gate and follow the farm track towards the woodland. Keep with the Heart of Wales Line through another gate and climb steadily between the trees. After around 1km, turn left on a forest road and continue for another 600m, before turning sharply left again. A path off to the right soon leads to the summit of Hopton Titterhill (397m). Over the top there are great views towards the

south Shropshire Hills, including Stiperstones, Caer Caradoc, The Lawley and The Wrekin, and the Clee Hills.

Continue on the path across a cleared area of the plantation and turn right to follow a section of mountain bike trail which twists and turns downhill; this section is used by riders coming slowly uphill but care should still be taken.

After around 2km, a forest track is reached and following a couple of bends the castle and village come into view. Exit the trees by a stile and continue over fields to reach the village via the stile in the hedge passed earlier.

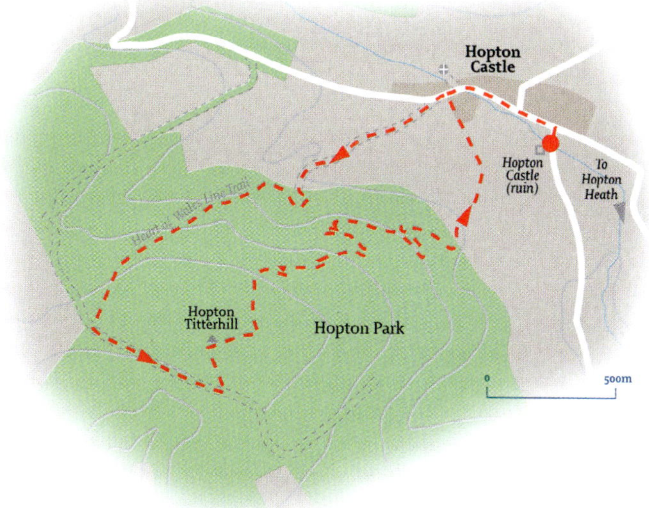

Knighton and Offa's Dyke

Distance 5.3km **Time** 1 hour 45
Terrain footpaths and forest tracks
Map OS Explorer 201 **Access** regular buses
to Knighton from Ludlow; trains from
Shrewsbury and Cardiff

Offa was the Anglo-Saxon King of Mercia
from 757 to 796AD who ordered that a dyke
be built to delineate the border between
his kingdom and Powys. This route
explores Kinsley Wood to the north of the
border town of Knighton before returning
on a section of the Offa's Dyke Path – the
285km-long trail which follows the route
of the dyke between Liverpool Bay and
the Severn Estuary. The walk finishes at
the volunteer-run Offa's Dyke Centre
which does excellent work promoting the
conservation and understanding of the
ancient earthwork.

The main visitor car park in Knighton
is by the livestock market, a short walk
from the railway station. If walking from
the car park, turn right on Station Road,
cross over the River Teme and then the
bridge over the railway before turning left
along Kinsley Road.

Look out for an unsigned and often
overgrown path leading into the trees off
to the right after about 200m. Although
this starts out as quite a rough path it
soon becomes clearer as it climbs into
Kinsley Wood to meet a forest road. Take
the road to the right and follow it around
the top of the plantation to the small car
park at the north end of the wood.

At the car park, bear left on the track for
a short distance, looking out for a path off
to the right after about 150m. Follow this
across a field to reach a marker post of the
Offa's Dyke Path, one of Britain's
National Trails. If you followed the trail
north from here for a few kilometres you
would get good views over Knighton and

◀ Crossing the border

the Knucklas Viaduct and reach Cwm-sanaham Hill (406m). The detour is well worth the effort on a clear day, although the path is fairly exposed and the hill requires a bit of a climb.

To complete this circuit, however, go left at the marker post and descend steeply along the edge of the plantation, then head through some woodland to return to Kinsley Road. Go over the road and pass Panpwnton Farm and campsite before crossing the railway and the River Teme. Follow the riverside path from here back into Knighton, looking out for some of the best remains of Offa's Dyke as you round the riverbend.

Protected as a scheduled monument, the earthwork was originally up to 20m wide and 2.4m high in places, and has great cultural significance, denoting the separation between England and Wales. As one Welsh historian has claimed, perhaps exaggerating a little, it was the custom for the English to slice off the ears of any Welshman found east of the dyke and 'for the Welsh to hang every Englishman found to the west of it'.

The path soon leads to the Offa's Dyke Centre where you can enjoy refreshments in the café and learn a bit more about the dyke before returning to the start.

Clun and Black Hill

Distance 10.3km **Time** 3 hours
Terrain forest tracks and footpaths
Map OS Explorer 201 **Access** regular buses
to Clun from Ludlow

Tucked away in a tranquil corner of
Shropshire, close to the border with
Wales, Clun is one of the 'quietest
places under the sun', according to
A E Housman's *A Shropshire Lad*. The
village is also popular with walkers
tackling the Shropshire Way or the Jack
Mytton Way, and among the town's many
attractions are a ruined Norman castle and
a 15th-century packhorse bridge still used
by traffic today. This walk follows country
roads after leaving the village, then
returns via a forest track with views over
the south Shropshire Hills.

Starting from the walkers' car park by
the Memorial Hall, head through town
to the packhorse bridge over the River
Clun and continue up Church Street
towards St George's Church. Bear left
along Vicarage Road, just before the
church, and then turn sharply right,
following the road signed for Woodside.
Continue on this road as it gently climbs
to arrive at a junction just past Woodside
Farm and the Old Farmhouse. Bear right
and carry on along the narrow road,
under the shade of the trees at first, until
you eventually arrive at a car park with
a Forestry Commission sign on the left
for Black Hill.

Head up the forestry track and take the
first left to continue to a junction. Go
right for a short distance at the junction,

then take the footpath on the left into the plantation.

The trig point for Black Hill is buried deep in the trees to the right of the path and can be accessed on a detour over rough ground through the tightly-planted conifers. If visiting the trig point is not your thing then keep on the path heading for the watchtower up ahead. Go left at the crossroads of firebreaks and right again on the forest track for 50m before heading left to soon meet another junction of tracks.

Continue straight on back into the tree cover and keep ahead again at the next junction, passing tall lichen-covered trees, to arrive at another track after a slightly steep section. Go left to follow this track which bends right into Sowdley Wood, then left, and leads back to Woodside.

Retrace the outward route along the road, looking out for a stile on the right, then cross a field to return to Clun via a ford. From the ford, continue through the town back to the start at the Memorial Hall or spend some time exploring the ruin of Clun Castle perched above the River Clun and overlooking the village.

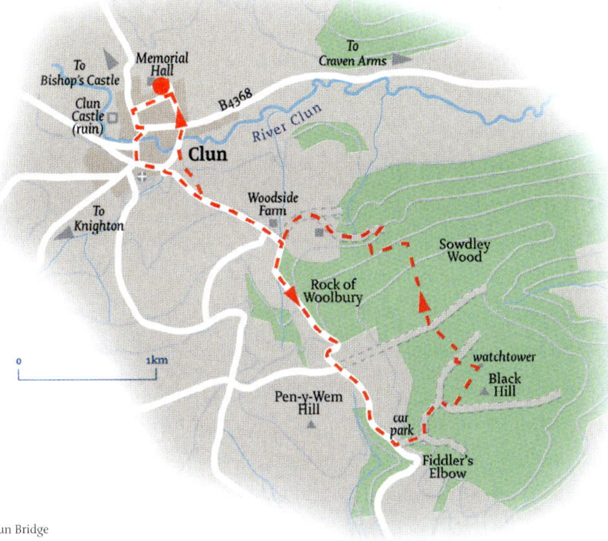

◄ Clun Bridge

Bishop's Castle and Oakeley Mynd

Distance 11km **Time** 3 hours 30
Terrain fields, footpaths and country
roads; several stiles **Map** OS Explorer 216
Access regular bus to Bishop's Castle
from Shrewsbury

Bishop's Castle sits at a junction of
old tracks once followed by travellers
and drovers taking livestock to market.
With its many fairs and festivals, it has
long had a reputation as a lively and
welcoming place. It is also home to
The Three Tuns Brewery, the oldest
licensed brewery in Britain, established
in 1642, and at one time the town was said
to have more than 40 pubs. The
Shropshire Way, the Kerry Ridgeway and
Offa's Dyke are all nearby and many
footpaths lead directly from the town
into the surrounding countryside for
expansive views of Shropshire.

The circular walk begins from the car
park of the livestock market in the centre
of town. Turn right down Station Street
and follow the footpath off the bend in
the road which leads through to Bowling
Green Close. Go left and continue on the
path at the end of the houses to reach
Love Lane on the edge of town.

Head straight over the road and go into
the field, continuing through another
couple of fields to arrive at the access road
for Oakeley Farm. Turn left and then right
soon after to follow a path up to Oakeley
Wood. Cross over the stiles and through
the woodland, with views north towards
Stiperstones and the southern end of the
Long Mynd as you make your way across
the flank of Oakeley Mynd.

Continue over fields and stiles, heading
for Home Farm and Totterton Hall to
meet an access track. Turn right and

◀ High Street, Bishop's Castle

follow the track out to the junction with Stank Lane. Cross over the lane and follow the permissive path to the village of Lydbury North (there is no Lydbury South) which is clearly seen up ahead. Keep left along the field edge as you approach the village to find a gate which leads onto Church Close and then Brampton Road.

Cross and turn right to pass St Michael & All Angels, then go up the lane by the side of the churchyard. Look out for a footpath between hedges at the end of the lane leading off behind the houses which brings you out near the village hall. Turn left, then follow Habershon Close up to the signposted bridleway which leads off to the left through the trees.

This section is quite rough in places as it passes Mears Barn and continues on a steady incline to reach a woodland. Carry on along the edge of fields to meet a farm road by Conery, then bear right to join Stank Lane. Go left to return to Bishop's Castle, following the pavement all the way to Love Lane and on to the town centre.

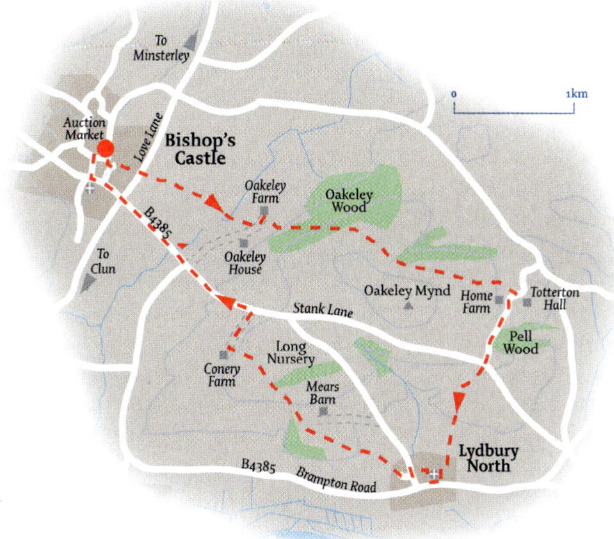

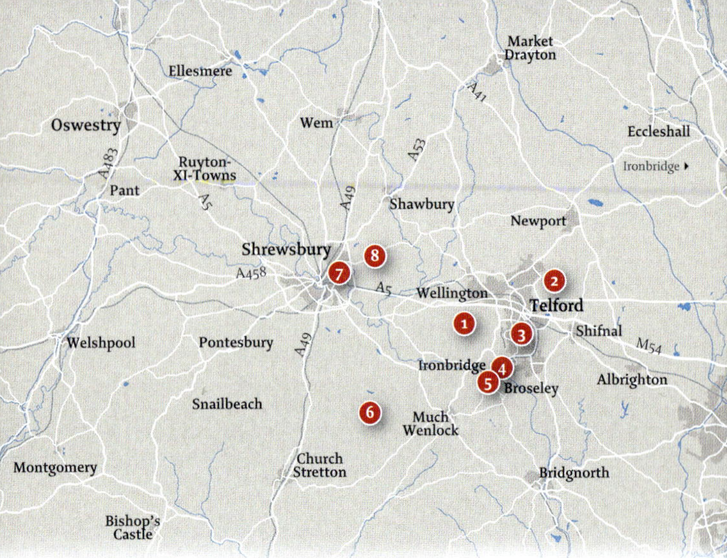

At the heart of Shropshire, sitting on a loop on the majestic River Severn and close to the Welsh border, the medieval town of Shrewsbury has always been an important place. The Welsh princes of Powys were the first to base themselves here in the 5th and 6th centuries, but Norman lords soon displaced them and established their own law and order over the Welsh Marches (the politically unstable area along the border), making the town their defensive and administrative stronghold. Trade in more peaceful times in Welsh wool and flax brought great prosperity and people, and today there are more than 600 listed buildings from the Tudor, Georgian and Regency periods in the town.

Downstream, the longest and most voluminous river in England and Wales, the Severn, passes under the world's first cast-iron bridge at the heart of a UNESCO World Heritage Site with a plethora of museums of industrial heritage nearby. This is where iron was first produced in coke-fuelled blast furnaces, a world-changing innovation that paved the way for the Industrial Revolution. An influx of workers – and profits for the bosses – changed the surrounding area forever, leaving behind rows of modest cottages, as well as fine country houses and estates.

Woodlands and wildflower meadows have taken the place of collieries and pit-heaps in more recent years, and bees, butterflies, willow tits and kingfishers have returned in number. The new town of Telford, named after the engineering genius, has also brought new energy and commercial innovation to the region.

Shrewsbury, Telford and Ironbridge

The Wrekin and The Ercall

Distance 14.8km **Time** 4 hours 30
Terrain footpaths, steep in places,
woodland **Map** OS Explorer 242
Access regular buses and trains to
Wellington from Shrewsbury

The highlight of this walk is the hillfort, built around 400BC by the Cornovii tribe, which crowns the summit of The Wrekin, Shropshire's 'beloved little mountain'. It's said that 17 counties can be seen from the top, as well as Wenlock Edge, the south Shropshire Hills and the Welsh hills. This longer route to the summit also takes in The Ercall, a neighbouring little hill well worth the extra effort.

Start from the car park at the leisure centre in Wellington, an historic market town with a bus and railway station. From the car park, turn left on Victoria Road, then go right down Tan Bank and look for a footpath beside the police station. This leads to New Church Road. Go right here and cross over Holyhead Road to Limekiln Lane on the left. Continue down the lane as it becomes a track going under the M54, then look out for a stile on the right and a path into Limekiln Wood.

Follow pink Telford T50 trail markers through the wood, passing the remains of old limekilns, and cross a meadow before going through woodland and meeting a rough track. Turn right on the track and continue across more meadow, turning right again at a T-junction. Keep on along the track and then bear left into woodland. Go through the trees to emerge on a road with the summit of The Wrekin up ahead.

Turn right and look out for steps leading off the road into woodland. The path crosses a field to the base of The Wrekin, then heads right to meet the

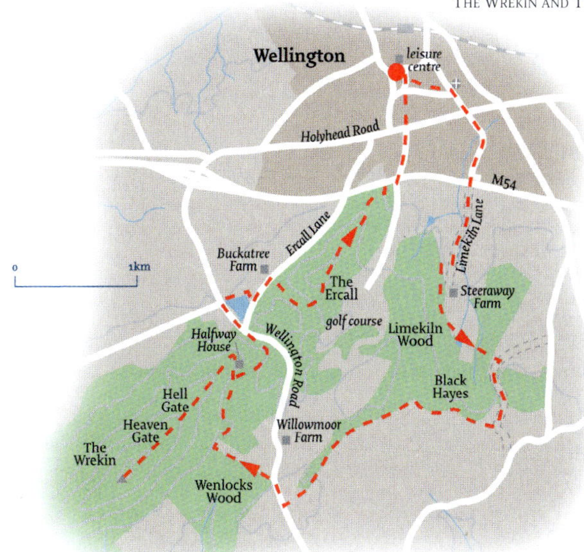

main track to the summit. The steepening track soon passes the Halfway House, which has a long history of serving tea and refreshments, and once offered donkey rides and hosted Saturday night dances for Victorian pleasure seekers.

Carry on up the track to the hillfort of Caer Uriconio, once home to a large Iron Age community. On the way to the summit you will pass through two earthen mounds – the first is Hell Gate, the outer entrance of the fort, and further up, Heaven Gate, the gateway to what was the fortified inner area. Once on top of the hill, there is a trig point, a toposcope and 360-degree views all around the county.

After exploring the summit, retrace your steps back down the hill but further down ignore the path that you came up on and keep to the main track all the way down. Go left for a short distance when you reach the road, then cross a stile leading onto a path that passes a small reservoir. This emerges on Ercall Lane where T50 trail markers guide you along the road for a short way and into The Ercall Nature Reserve on the steep flank of The Ercall. This ancient oak woodland, looked after by the Shropshire Wildlife Trust, is usually quieter than The Wrekin and a pleasure to walk through.

Come down off the hill to emerge on Golf Links Lane which goes under the M54 to meet Holyhead Road. A footpath on the other side of the road leads back to Tarn Bank and the car park at the start.

Granville to the Lilleshall Monument

Distance 9km **Time** 2 hours 30
Terrain footpaths, woodland, fields, short
climb to monument **Map** OS Explorer 242
Access regular buses to Donnington from
Telford town centre

The blast furnaces, coalmines and canals
are long gone from Granville, replaced
by the flower-filled meadows, wet
woodlands and marshy pools that make
up this sprawling country park on the
edge of Telford. This walk explores the
old industrial site before taking in a
landmark monument to local landowner
and one of the wealthiest men of the 19th
century, the 1st Duke of Sutherland.

Start from the signposted car park off
Granville Road and take the steps up to
'the Top of the World' viewpoint on
what used to be a pit-mound when this
area was a hive of industry. Continue to
drop back down to the main path and
pass the remains of old stone and brick
colliery buildings as you make your way
to Waxhill Meadow and Muxton Lane.

Go left on the lane, looking out for a
stile marked by the pink Telford T50 trail
roundel. Go through a couple of
hedgerows and cross the field with the
Lilleshall Monument now visible up
ahead. After arriving at Lilyhurst Road,
turn left and take care as you head
towards the village and turn up Church
Road. Continue past the Church of
St Michael and some houses, then follow
a signed footpath behind a hedge off to
the left which emerges on a narrow lane
on the hillside.

Go right along the lane, passing the
rear of houses, to arrive at the foot of
the steep footpath to the monument.
Make your way to the top for views of

The Wrekin and further afield. The monument is a 21m-high stone obelisk erected in 1833 which commemorates George Granville Leveson-Gower, 1st Duke of Sutherland. Described as a 'leviathan of wealth', the duke owned extensive lands in Staffordshire, Yorkshire and the Scottish Highlands, as well as Shropshire, and remains a controversial figure for his role in carrying out the notorious Highland Clearances where thousands of his tenants were evicted to make way for more profitable sheep farms and rehoused in coastal communities.

The route off the hill is opposite the ascent. Once back on the lane, carry on downhill and through the churchyard to return to Church Road. Retrace your steps to Lilyhurst Road and across the field,

bearing right as you approach Muxton Lane. The route then follows the T50 trail markers past Muxton Primary School, back into the woodland and up some steep steps heading towards Muxton Marsh. Just before the marsh, bear left towards Granville Country Park. Cross the road and follow the path left up a short incline to meet the main path which leads back to the car park.

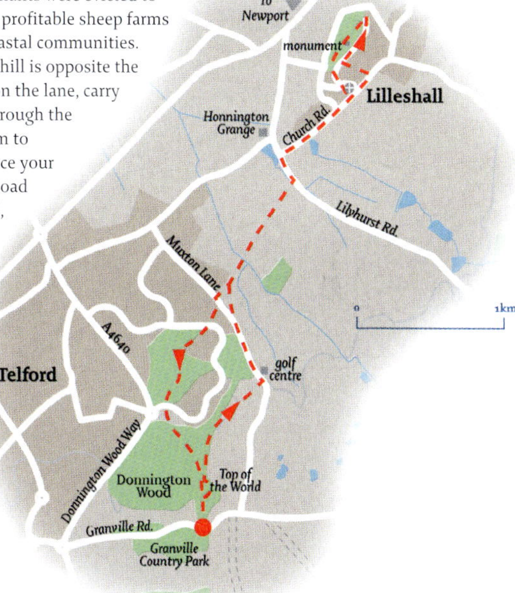

Telford Town Park and Heritage Trail

Distance 7km **Time** 1 hour 45
Terrain woodland paths, mostly flat
Map OS Explorer 242 **Access** regular buses
from Telford town centre; trains from
Shrewsbury and Birmingham to Telford
Central Station, 1.5km from the start

Planned in the 1970s as a 'green lung'
for the residents of the new town of
Telford, the popular Town Park attracts
thousands of visitors from far and wide
who come to enjoy its many attractions.
This walk explores the southern end of
the park where pools, pit mounds,
woodlands and meadows surround the
impressive Stirchley Chimney, a reminder
of the industry that once existed here.
The mosaic of habitats that have
developed since support a great variety
of wildlife.

Begin the walk from the visitor centre
and follow the Heritage Trail past the
walls of the old Norman chapel, once part
of an estate that was swallowed up by the
new town development, towards the high
ropes course.

Continue on through what was once the
site of Randlay Brickworks on a path
which follows the line of the old mineral
railway line that carried raw materials and
other goods to and from the industrial
works. The Blue Pool to the left was once
a quarry for the brickworks.

At the next junction keep right to arrive
at a crossroads of paths and go left,
following the cast-iron 'Twin Tracks'
artwork designed by local children in
tribute to Thomas Telford, the Scottish
engineering titan that the planned new
town was named after. After passing the
Jubilee Column, the path continues
around beneath the 64m-high Stirchley
Chimney, which was integral to the
ironworks that operated here.

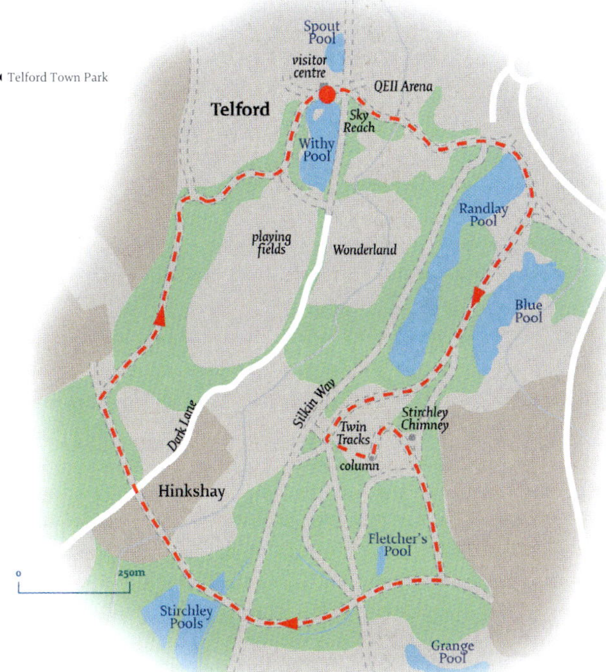

◄ Telford Town Park

Carry on along the Heritage Trail towards Fletcher's Pool and Grange Pool, which can be visited off the main path. At the junction take the second left towards Stirchley Pools and Hinkshay village.

At the next crossroads the Heritage Trail follows the Silkin Way to the right which leads back to the start. The Silkin Way is a traffic-free walking and cycling route which runs all the way to Ironbridge following the original route of the Coalport Branch of the London and North Western Railway Line. The old platform of Stirchley Station can be visited on a short detour to the left.

To extend the walk, continue on the Nature Trail straight ahead. This leads between some houses and crosses a road before bearing right and weaving through woodland and heath to arrive back at Withy Pool just to the south of the visitor centre and the start.

Ironbridge and Coalport

Distance 9.5km **Time** 2 hours
Terrain footpaths, undulating woodland;
some steep steps **Map** OS Explorer 242
Access regular buses to Ironbridge from
Telford and Shrewsbury

A UNESCO World Heritage site with an array of fascinating museums, the village of Ironbridge takes its name from the 30m-long cast-iron bridge which was raised over the gorge of the River Severn in 1779. This peaceful undulating walk tours an area where the sound of furnaces, factories, foundries and workshops would once have been deafening, before returning to the bridge, a proud reminder of the ingenuity of the industrial age.

From the tollhouse on the south side of the bridge, walk through the car park, the old station yard, following the Telford T50 trail and the Severn Way. Remnants of the railway can be seen alongside the track and on the north side of the river the remains of the iron-smelting Bedlam Furnaces soon come into view. Keep on along the path through the railway gates and continue on the pavement to the Jackfield Tile Museum which tells the story of Britain's decorative tile industry.

Further along the path is a riverside pub and restaurant and Maws Craft Centre, a former tile factory, where you can detour through the courtyard. The T50 trail soon turns off and crosses the river by a footbridge next to the Boat Inn but keep on the Severn Way to reach Coalport Bridge. Originally made of wood, the bridge was replaced by cast iron in 1818 and is still open to light traffic.

Once across, go left to follow the Silkin Way, named after Lewis Silkin, the government minister responsible for the New Towns Act of 1946, into woodland and pass the Brewery Inn. Further on, it is

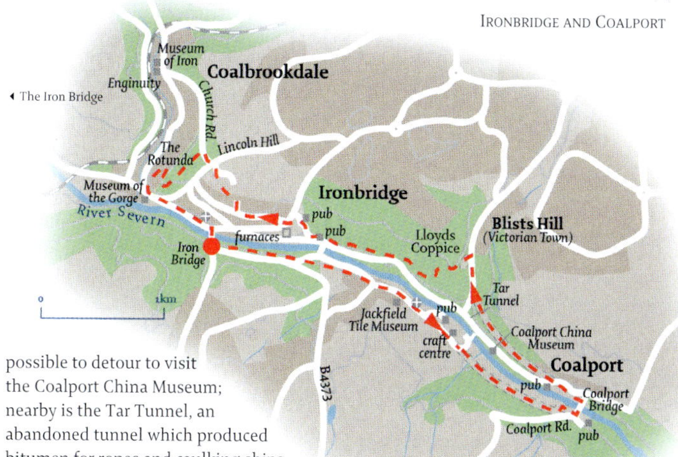

possible to detour to visit the Coalport China Museum; nearby is the Tar Tunnel, an abandoned tunnel which produced bitumen for ropes and caulking ships.

The path continues across the Hay Inclined Plane, which once carried coal and iron up to the Shropshire Canal via a pair of wooden tub boats, towards the Blists Hill Victorian Town, an open-air living history museum. At the rear entrance to Blists Hill, cross the road to pick up the T50 trail again, past some houses, and enter the woodland of Lloyds Coppice. Take care on the steep steps as you follow the lower path through the woods to emerge on the road to Ironbridge. Follow this to the towering steel bridge which replaced the innovative concrete 'Free Bridge'.

Soon after this, go right up Newbridge Road and bear left at the Golden Ball Inn down a lane to cross the main road into Ironbridge. Continue up Belmont Road and along Hodge Bower before turning right up a lane which leads onto a footpath. After enjoying views over the gorge, go through a gate and down the lane to cross over to Church Road. This goes to the Victorian Coalbrookdale Inn, the Museum of Iron, and Enginuity, an interactive design and technology centre, but this route continues along a footpath on the left to visit Lincoln Hill, formerly a vast limestone quarry, and The Rotunda, site of a long-gone circular structure built in the 1790s with a revolving seat allowing panoramic views over the gorge and The Wrekin. The paths here were first laid out between 1782 and 1792 by Richard Reynolds, an ironmaster who wanted to create 'Sabbath Walks' as a healthier alternative to the alehouse for his men at the end of the long working week.

Continue carefully down the steps to reach Paradise and carry on to the main road to visit the riverside Museum of the Gorge, or go along the Wharfage, with its many shops and cafés, to cross over the Iron Bridge and return to the start.

Broseley and Benthall Hall

Distance 5.3km **Time** 1 hour 30
Terrain footpaths and pavements
Map OS Explorer 242 **Access** regular buses
to Broseley from Telford

The town of Broseley sits on the south
bank of the Ironbridge Gorge and shares
much of the industrial history of its better
known neighbour. This circular walk
around the former pipe-making and iron-
smelting centre, which expanded
massively to accommodate a growing
workforce during the industrial age, can
be combined with a visit to Benthall Hall,
a fine 16th-century country house on the
plateau above the gorge.

Start from the Memorial Gardens and
walk up to the junction at the top of the
High Street, then bear left following the
sign for Benthall Hall. Carry on over
Barratt's Hill, passing one of the scrap-
iron artworks on the town's sculpture
trail, and turn down Speed's Lane.

Look for a gate in the hedge and cross
Penn's Meadow to Bridge Bank, then
follow the waymarked path which goes
through to a lane. Turn right and follow
this to the old farm buildings, then go
left along a grassy path which eventually
leads to the handsome Elizabethan manor
house of Benthall Hall.

The National Trust property has been
home to the Benthall family since the 11th
century and saw some skirmishing in the
Civil War when it was garrisoned by the
Parliamentarians. The adjoining Church of
St Bartholomew was destroyed in the war
and rebuilt in 1667 after the Restoration.
The Benthalls had private Catholic
sympathies and the house has several
secret hiding places for religious items.

To return to Broseley, pick up the path
again opposite the visitor car park and
keep straight on to reach a walkers' gate
at a junction of paths. Turn right and in
400m bear right again down the joining

◄ Benthall Hall

lane at The Mines. A narrow footpath soon leads off the lane, crosses a meadow and bears left to re-emerge between houses on Bridge Bank. Carry on down the lane on the opposite side of the road to reach Simpson's Lane. Turn right and continue to pass a sign for Lloyds Jitty, one of the many narrow passageways in Broseley which run between workers' cottages. A little further on is another jitty, the Ding Dong Steps, which got its name from the sound of clogs ringing on the stone steps set between high walls.

At the end of the lane go left up steepening Legges Hill and turn right at the top. Go along King Street and bear left by the garage along Duke Street to soon arrive at the old Broseley Pipeworks. This is the former home of one of the largest clay tobacco pipe makers in the world. The fragile pipes were popular from the first imports of tobacco in the 16th century to the introduction of cigarettes at the end of the 19th century. As well as pipes, the local potters made tavern mugs for thirsty miners and watermen who looked after the export of coal down the River Severn.

From the pipeworks, carry on down Duke Street to return to the High Street and the Memorial Gardens at the start.

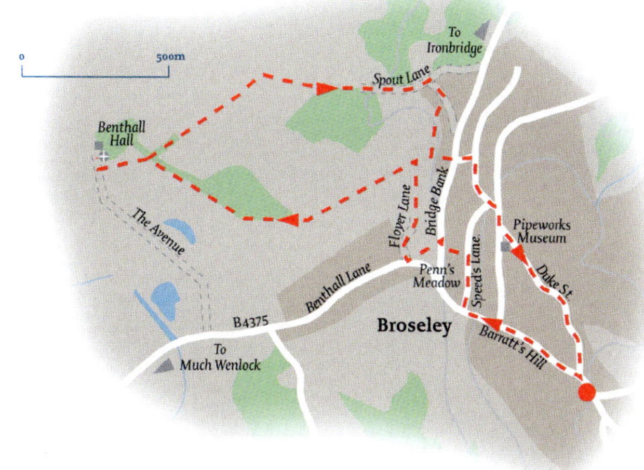

Acton Burnell and Langley Chapel

Distance 8.7km **Time** 2 hours 30 **Terrain** footpaths, road, farm tracks and fields **Maps** OS Explorer 241 and 217 **Access** regular buses to Acton Burnell from Shrewsbury

In the autumn of 1283, King Edward I held the first Parliament of England in which commoners as well as lords were represented in a tithe barn in Acton Burnell. The nearby fortified manor house known as Acton Burnell Castle was built by Robert Burnell, Bishop of Bath and Wells, and is the start point for this circuit of the surrounding countryside.

From St Mary's Church, adjacent to the castle, follow the path south through a short wooded section to a stile and go left along the side of a field until you reach the road at another stile.

At the road, turn left and continue towards the hamlet of Ruckley with distant views towards The Lawley, Caer Caradoc and the Long Mynd in the Shropshire hills. As the road rounds a bend, a short detour left takes you to the austere but enchanting Langley Chapel, one of the few new churches built in the Elizabethan period. Looked after by English Heritage, the chapel still has the original 17th-century wooden pews.

After returning to the Ruckley road, continue past Ruckley Hall Farm and take the signed bridleway off to the right. Follow this as it turns left, then right and go through Lodgehill Coppice on a forestry track. At the end of the track, bear right to pass Frodesley Lodge and continue on the farm track all the way to the little village of Frodesley.

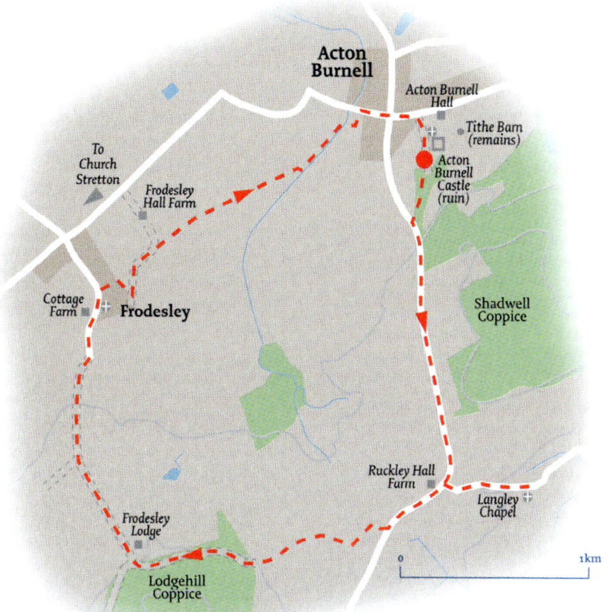

Just past St Mark's Church, turn right onto a bridleway and pick up the track which leads towards Frodesley Hall Farm. (follow the waymarked path which avoids the farm itself). Continue in the direction of The Wrekin which can be seen in the distance, crossing fields and going over stiles. If crops are growing in the field then it may be better to go around the edge of the field to reach a track which soon meets the road into Acton Burnell.

Turn right on the road and pass the post office and village shop to return to Acton Burnell Castle. This road also leads to Concord College, an international school centred around the classical Acton Burnell Hall, built in the early 19th century by the Smythe family.

The ruins of Robert Burnell's old sandstone castle, behind the church, are partly shaded by a magnificent Cedar of Lebanon tree and not far away, the remaining gable end walls of the 'barn that changed history' can be seen in the college grounds.

◄ Acton Burnell Castle

Shrewsbury and Uffington

Distance 11.5km **Time** 2 hours 45 **Terrain** pavements, riverside footpaths and cyclepath **Map** OS Explorer 241 **Access** Shrewsbury is well served by buses and trains

Encircled by a loop of the River Severn, Shrewsbury's town centre is almost an island with a medieval street plan and hundreds of listed buildings, many with timber framing and dating from the 15th and 16th centuries. This walk follows the Shropshire Way and a section of cyclepath which shadows the old Shropshire canal to visit the outlying village of Uffington.

From the magnificent Tudor-style railway station, turn right and go beneath the railway bridge, heading right again along Howard Street to reach Shrewsbury Prison. Decommissioned in 2013 and now a state-of-the art visitor attraction, the Victorian prison building is built on the site of the medieval Dana Gaol and is still known as The Dana.

Take the footbridge over the railway opposite the prison and bear left on the path that leads around the side of the red sandstone Shrewsbury Castle. Built by William I in the 11th century as an administrative centre and a defensive

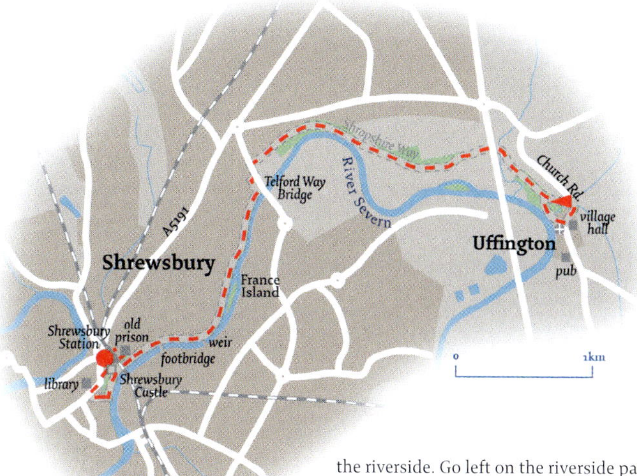

fortification for the town, the castle sits on a hill in the neck of the meander of the river. Town walls were also built in response to Welsh raids, although Llywelyn the Great, Prince of Wales, managed to take the castle briefly in 1215.

The path emerges on Castle Gates, opposite the town library, with an impressive statue of Charles Darwin, naturalist and father of evolutionary theory, ahead. Born in Shrewsbury in 1809, Darwin attended a local school before going on to university in Edinburgh and Cambridge, and setting sail on HMS *Beagle* and circumnavigating the globe.

Pass the library and continue along the shopping street before turning left down Windsor Place and immediately left again down St Mary's Water Lane which leads to

the riverside. Go left on the riverside path, following the Shropshire Way under the railway bridge and on past the Castle Walk footbridge and a weir. A section of road follows before the path continues under a roadbridge. This riverside section can be overgrown and muddy, so a better alternative is to detour left to pick up the cyclepath a short distance away and cross over the Telford Way road.

Continue on the cyclepath, which runs alongside the old Shrewsbury Canal all the way to Uffington. Just before arriving in the village, however, follow the Shropshire Way out to the main road through the village. This comes out at the village hall, with the local pub a short distance down the road to the right.

To return to Shrewsbury, go back along the short section of the Shropshire Way or pick up the start of the cyclepath a little distance along the road.

◀ Charles Darwin statue in front of Shrewsbury Library

Haughmond Hill and Abbey

Distance 7.25km **Time** 2 hours 30
Terrain footpaths, undulating woodland,
short road section **Map** OS Explorer 241
Access no public transport to the start

Haughmond Abbey was an Augustinian
monastery to the east of Shrewsbury
which became one of the great medieval
abbeys of England thanks to the support
of the wealthy Fitzalan family. This walk
visits the extensive ruins after exploring
some of the trails in the nearby forest
and climbing Haughmond Hill, 'yon
bosky hill' over which the blood-red sun
rose on the morning of the Battle of
Shrewsbury in 1403, according to
Shakespeare (*Henry IV, Part 1*).

Start from Forestry England's
Haughmond Hill car park (charge) off the
B5062 Newport Road where there is a café
and toilets. Take the path with the blue
markers (Wilfred's Walk) which is well
laid and pleasantly winds through

woodland to the edge of the forest area.
There is one right turn to look out for
where the yellow marked trail branches
off on a shorter route, but keep following
the blue markers to the edge of the fields
and views towards The Wrekin.

From the viewpoint, keep with the blue
markers along the forest track and go left
to loop around to Haughmond Hill's trig
point (153m) and return to the forest track.
Continue on the track from here to the
main viewpoint and the toposcope on the
rocky summit with clear views over
Shrewsbury and the south Shropshire
hills on a clear day. Known as Douglas's
Leap, this is said to be where Lord
Archibald, 4th Earl of Douglas, fell from
his horse while fleeing Henry IV's men
following the Battle of Shrewsbury
between the king and rebels led by Henry
'Harry Hotspur' Percy in 1403.

A sham castle, built in the late 18th
century, also once stood nearby to serve

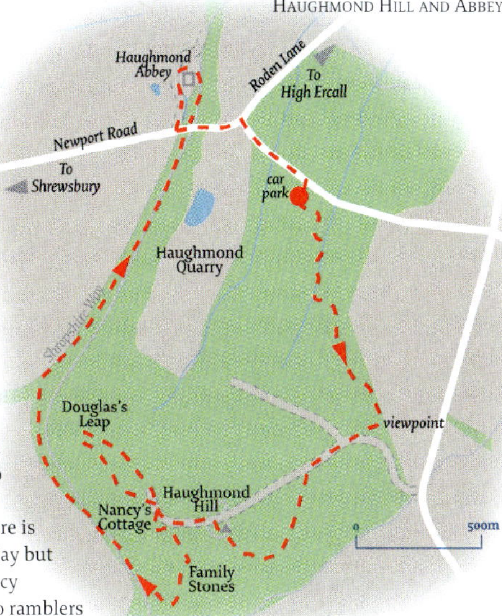

◀ Haughmond Abbey

as an 'eye-catcher' and a 'refreshment pavilion' for huntsmen. Sadly it collapsed in the 1930s and only a few pieces of masonry remain.

From the viewpoint, loop back to the main forest path and after a short distance go off to the right to the site of Nancy Spragg's cottage. There is little left of the building today but up to her death in 1904, Nancy served teas and lemonade to ramblers from her simple hillside abode here. Continue to the Family Stones viewpoint where there are a couple of benches and views towards The Wrekin.

Take the path to the left of the benches down a short, fairly steep section which can be overgrown and muddy depending on the season. Go right at the next junction and carry on to join the Shropshire Way as it heads north to the Newport Road and Haughmond Abbey.

On the way, the route passes below a knoll on the hill known as Queen Eleanor's Bower. It is said that Henry IV's wife watched over his victory at the Battle of Shrewsbury from here. Confusingly, however, his wife at the time was called Joan, not Eleanor. The Bower is more likely to have been named after Eleanor of Aquitaine, wife of Henry II, who was famously imprisoned by her husband after she plotted against him.

Carefully cross the road and turn left to reach the entrance to the abbey, an English Heritage site with no charge for entry. Following Henry VIII's Dissolution of the Monasteries in 1539, the abandoned abbey was converted into a Tudor mansion with courtyards and a walled garden. By the 18th century, however, the site was again a ruin but maintained by the Corbet family of nearby Sundorne House, the new owners, as a romantic feature for their extensive garden.

Loop around the abbey site, returning to the road on the Shropshire Way before heading back to the forest car park.

Where Shropshire meets the West Midlands and the more industrial Black Country (named after the grimy iron, steel, coal and cokeworks) is still a largely rural area full of neat villages, twisting lanes, working farms and old woods.

Reminders of a more industrial past are never far away, however – the Severn Valley Railway heritage line from Kidderminster to Bridgnorth is a great way to get around, several sections of abandoned canal have been brought back to life and on either side of the Severn at Highley old colliery land has been reclaimed for recreation.

Also straddling the river, the town of Bridgnorth was a favourite of the luckless King Charles I, and his son, the future Charles II, made his escape from Cromwell's patrols through the countryside around here, hiding in hedgerows and, famously, in the branches of an old oak tree. Also popular with royalty, the charming Much Wenlock grew up around the priory founded by King Merewalh of Mercia in the 7th century, although visitors today are just as likely to make a pilgrimage to the nearby limestone escarpment of Wenlock Edge, formerly a coral reef in a subtropical sea.

Newport Canal ▶

East Shropshire

Newport and Edgmond

Distance 12km **Time** 3 hours
Terrain pavement, footpaths, fields
Maps OS Explorer 242 and 243
Access buses to Newport from Telford

Newport is a busy market town near the Shropshire and Staffordshire border, not far from the Aqualate Mere, the largest natural lake in the English Midlands. This walk follows a section of the old Newport Canal for a tour of the surrounding countryside before returning through the village of Edgmond.

The walk begins from the Water Lane car park by the truncated Newport Canal. Not connected to the main canal network, the Newport waterway was abandoned in 1944 and most of it filled in, but it is slowly being brought back to life by the Shrewsbury and Newport Canals Trust, which was set up with the goal of creating a continuous waterway linking the Shropshire Union Canal to Shrewsbury once again.

Go over the bridge and drop down to the towpath opposite the car park, then follow it past the canal basin, the town's original wharfage. Continue to go under the Summer House Bridge to reach Meretown Lock No 18 just before the A41 Newport Bypass. Carry straight on along a grassy path which soon turns left to join a lane – this goes between some houses to Forton Road. Cross over and go through the gap in the hedge before turning right to walk around the rugby fields.

Once at the far end of the pitches, go right to head through woodland and soon reach Chester Road. Take care crossing the road and follow the pavement past the end of Park Pool and on to St Michael and All Angels Church. Immediately after

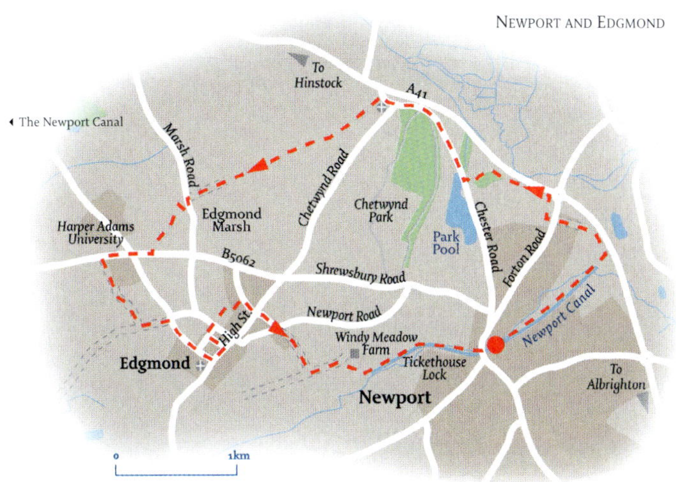

the church, there is a path off to the left along the edge of the field, just before the road joins the A41. Follow this around four fields before joining an access track which leads to Edgmond Marsh, just north of Edgmond. The village is thought to have been founded by a Danish settler called Eckmund on higher ground above the boggy marshland.

Turn left on the road and then right to follow a signposted path between houses which re-emerges on Shrewsbury Road near the entrance of the Harper Adams University, which specialises in higher education for the agricultural and rural sector. Go right past the university entrance and the entrance to the Veterinary Education centre before crossing the road to follow a gravel track which goes around some industrial buildings and a field. Go left after the field to join Flatt Road, turning right to

follow Hillside and then School Road to Edgmond's High Street.

Turn right for a short detour to visit St Peter's Church or go left to continue along the High Street to the war memorial before going left up Manor Road. Go right at the end of the lane on the path alongside Pipers Lane to meet Stackyard Lane. Carry on along the signposted path to Shrewsbury Road, then turn right to pass the village hall and the Methodist chapel to arrive at the High Street again.

Continue down Newport Road to a bend in the road and keep straight on down the track which runs behind the houses. At the next junction, turn left and go towards Windy Meadow Farm. Bear right before the farm to follow the path across the field which rejoins the Newport Canal at the old Tickethouse Lock. Follow the canalside path back to the start from here.

Shifnal and King Charles's Wood

Distance 11km **Time** 3 hours
Terrain pavement, tracks, paths, fields,
country road **Map** OS Explorer 242
Access regular buses to Shifnal from
Telford and Wolverhampton

**King Charles II famously hid from a patrol
of Parliamentarian soldiers inside a
pollarded oak tree in the grounds of
Boscobel House after his defeat at the
Battle of Worcester in 1651, the last major
battle of the English Civil War. This walk
explores the woodland south of the
market town of Shifnal through which the
king made his way to an aborted crossing
of the River Severn before he finally
escaped England via the south coast to
begin his long exile in France.**

From the railway station in Shifnal,
cross the road and go down Church Street.
Follow the road past St Andrew's Church,

Shifnal's parish church, part of which
dates from the 12th century, and on to the
roundabout. Carry on heading out of
town on the Telford road before turning
left onto the long private drive to 15th-
century Shifnal Manor.

Pass Mill Cottage and go right when the
driveway splits, making your way around
the farm buildings and along the field
edges to enter woodland. The path
emerges from the trees to join a track,
then carries on to pass a footbridge.
Continue south, following Wesley Brook,
to arrive at Evelith Mill, an old cornmill
which ceased working in the 1930s.

Turn left on the road and then right into
King Charles's Wood. The defeated king
passed through here on his way from
White Ladies Priory as he attempted to
cross the River Severn at Madeley. It is
said he was forced to run down the lane

◀ Evelith Mill and Millhouse

and jump behind a hedge after being challenged by the miller at Evelith. Finding his escape route to the Welsh coast blocked by Cromwell's patrols, he returned, exhausted and in tatters, to hide in the branches of an oak tree at Boscobel House before making his way south to Shoreham and on to Paris.

At the end of the track, bear right to cross a small bridge and sluice to reach Kemberton Mill, then follow the footpath sign by the cottages through the gate into the field. Continue across the fields, crossing a number of stiles to reach Kemberton Gorse, a steep-sided valley with steps down, then up again to a meadow. Cross the stile into the woods and continue to Grindleforge, then turn left to cross the bridge and follow the road up the hill past the old brewery building. After a few hundred metres, turn left into a hedged driveway towards Hinnington Grange. At the end of the drive, go past the farm buildings through a gate and along a track. The path turns left at some cottages into a field to return to Kemberton Mill.

Retrace the path through King Charles's Wood to Evelith Mill and continue on the marked footpath past the mill buildings.

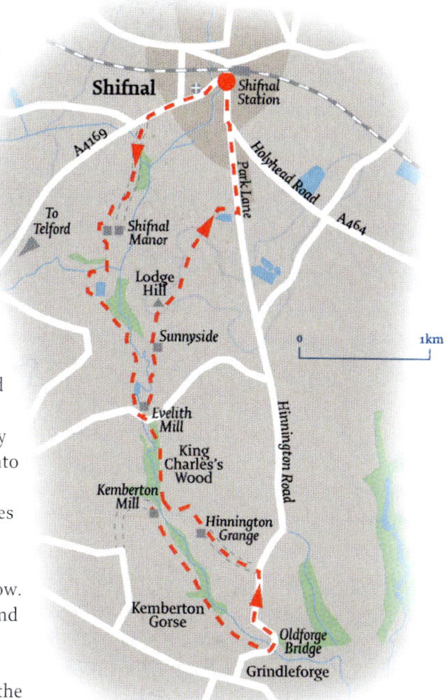

Follow the path through woodland and fields, and continue past the farm buildings at Sunnyside. Cross a stile and climb a small hill to take in the view over the Shropshire countryside towards the Clee Hills. A little further on and Shifnal will come into view as you continue on the path to Park Lane which leads back to the station.

Tong and White Ladies Priory

Distance 14.6km **Time** 3 hours 30
Terrain footpaths and pavement; some
country roads and farm tracks
Map OS Explorer 242 **Access** regular buses
to Albrighton from Telford; trains from
Telford, Shrewsbury and Wolverhampton

The Monarch's Way is a 1006km long-distance footpath which loosely follows the route taken by King Charles II in 1651 as he evaded capture by Cromwell's Roundheads following his defeat at the Battle of Worcester. This walk follows a short section which takes in the White Ladies Priory, one of the places he sought refuge, and passes the site of Hubbal Grange, the home of a servant family who risked their lives to save the king.

Start from the railway station in Albrighton, close to RAF Cosford and the RAF Museum Midlands. Exit on Station Road, go under the railway bridge and take care crossing the A41 bypass. Keep straight on down the road, then go left as the road turns right and continue past a row of trees to a stile opposite the pond.

Cross over the field to a small footbridge and go across another field to Donington Lane. A quick right, then left turn on the lane takes you to another path across fields with views towards The Wrekin and the unmistakable silver building which houses part of the RAF Museum at Cosford.

At the end of this field, bear left, then right into Mill Lane, a road which passes RAF housing. Go through the estate gate and follow the road past a pond and under the M54, then bear left to join the access track to Tong Park Farm. Continue along the road running alongside the motorway and then the A41 to enter the village of Tong with the imposing St Bartholomew's Church up ahead.

The graveyard here is where you'll find the grave of Little Nell from Charles

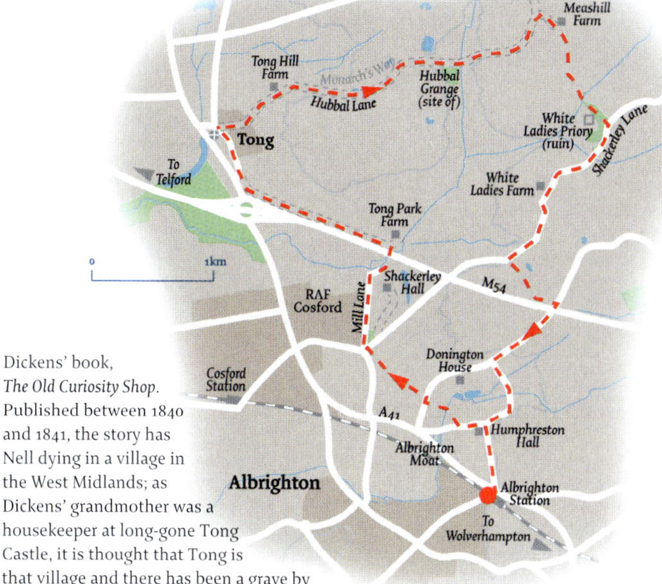

Dickens' book, *The Old Curiosity Shop*. Published between 1840 and 1841, the story has Nell dying in a village in the West Midlands; as Dickens' grandmother was a housekeeper at long-gone Tong Castle, it is thought that Tong is that village and there has been a grave by the church since 1910.

Leave Tong by Hubbal Lane across from the church and follow the Monarch's Way past Tong Hill Farm to the site of Hubbal Grange, now covered in trees, to the side of the track. King Charles II rested here during his escape and was tended to by Richard Penderel who cut his hair short, disguised him as a humble woodsman and covered his face with soot.

The path continues towards Meashill Farm and passes through the farmyard to exit on the other side on a path leading towards White Ladies Priory. Formerly a small nunnery of 'white ladies' or Augustinian canonesses, it is better known as the place where a desperate King Charles first sought refuge after his defeat at Worcester. Although 3000 of his Scottish troops under General Leslie were gathered at nearby Tong Castle, the Roundheads were closing in and his options for escape to Wales or Scotland were quickly being closed off.

From the priory, continue to Shackerley Lane and turn right to pass White Ladies Farm. Further on, take a left onto a farm track which goes past a large storage shed before joining a lane. Cross over the M54 and continue to a junction where you turn left onto Cordy Lane. Follow this round to the bypass and return to the station.

◀ White Ladies Priory

Badger and the Dingle

Distance 4km **Time** 1 hour
Terrain country roads, woodland paths,
fields **Map** OS Explorer 218 **Access** regular
buses to Badger from Telford and Shifnal

The small hamlet of Badger, and the
nearby landscaped wilderness garden
designed by William Emes, a pupil of
Capability Brown, in the late 18th century,
is a hidden gem on the edge of
Shropshire. This walk tours the woods
and farmland around the village before
returning through the stream-cut ravine
of Badger Dingle.

Somewhat off the beaten track, Badger
is best reached by bus as there is very
little room to park. To start the walk, head
north from the bus stop, out of the village
along Badger Lane. Once around the bend
follow the signposted track between trees
opposite the driveway to Badger Hall.
The original grand Georgian manor house

of Badger Hall was sadly demolished in
the 1950s, although its service buildings
were retained and refurbished.

Follow the forest track past a turn-off
which leads to Beckbury and continue to
meet the road just outside Stableford.
This village was home to the writer and
humorist P G Wodehouse in his teenage
years and the local villages frequently
featured in his comic novels. Badger
Dingle became Badgwick Dingle, for
example, and Ackleton became Eckleton,
although it is not known exactly which
country pile inspired Blandings Castle,
home of amiable Lord Emsworth and his
prize pig, the Empress of Blandings.

Just over the stone bridge before the
village, take the path left through a gate
and follow it to cross the River Worfe.
Climb up through the field to the top of a
small hill and carry on to join Stableford
Road towards Ackleton. After passing

◄ Town Pool in Badger

some houses, turn left on the signposted bridleway which leads to Badger Dingle.

Listed Grade II in Historic England's Register of Parks and Gardens, the Dingle contains a network of paths, as well as several pools, a waterfall, an icehouse, a rotunda and red sandstone caves. All around there are specimen trees such as Wellingtonia, yew, box, oak, beech and pine, and when the Dingle was first opened to the public in 1851 it was a popular place for factory outings from Wolverhampton and Birmingham.

A summerhouse, originally with a small banqueting room and a basement kitchen, also sits above the ravine. Known at different times as the Doric Temple, the Birdhouse or the Pigeon House, it was designed by the great architect James Wyatt for the owner of the estate, the industrialist Isaac Hawkins Browne. After spending many years as an empty folly, it was restored in the 1990s and is now managed by the Landmark Trust as a holiday let.

After exploring the Dingle return to Badger on a path which emerges on the road just south of the village.

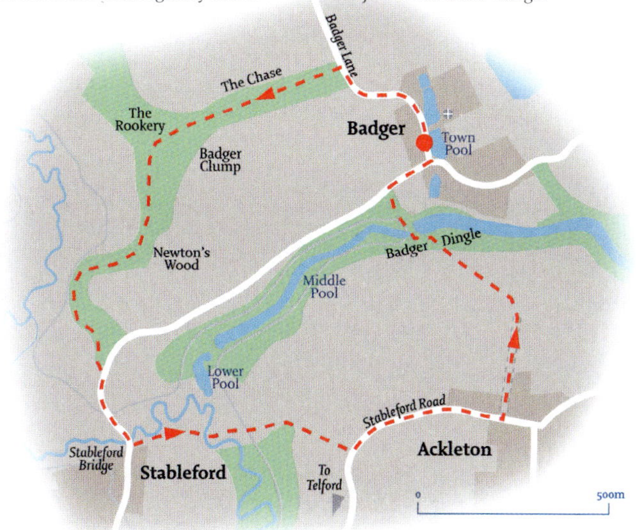

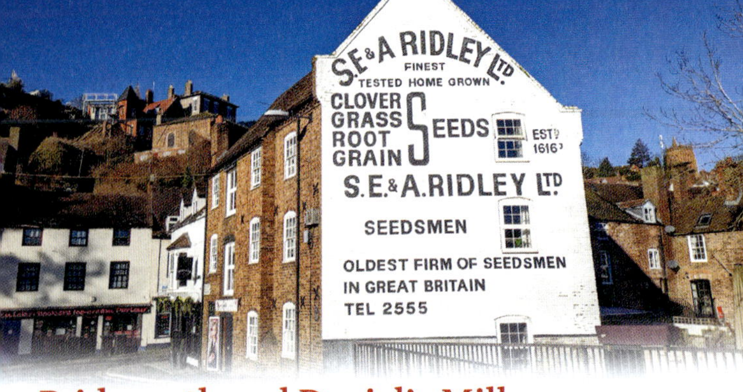

Bridgnorth and Daniel's Mill

Distance 12km **Time** 3 hours
Terrain footpaths, fields and pavements
Map OS Explorer 218 **Access** regular buses
to Bridgnorth from Telford

Split by the longest river in Britain into
the Low Town on the left bank and the
High Town on the right bank, Bridgnorth
was a favourite of King Charles I, who
remarked in 1642 that the view from the
top of the sandstone cliff over the River
Severn below was 'the finest in my
domain'. This walk follows the river
before looping back to the High Town and
passing beneath the ruined castle on the
clifftop to return to the river.

The walk begins in Low Town on the
east side of the River Severn. Head over
the bridge towards High Town and the
S E & A Ridley Ltd signage on the side of
the building. Bear left along the pavement
and pick up the path heading south
alongside the river. At times the river may
be high enough to flood this path.

Continue under the bypass bridge on
the Severn Way footpath before taking a
short detour along the pavement to pass
Daniel's Mill, a working watermill with
the largest cast-iron waterwheel used for
milling flour in England. Return to the
riverside path and, shortly after passing
through woodland, go right when the
path splits towards the sewage works,
then bear right, climbing away from the
river to join Slade Lane. Follow this, then
bear right at a small woodland to pass a
white cottage and cross over the railway
line. Continue into Eardington and turn
left to walk through the village to
Eardington Nature Reserve.

This site occupies an old quarry which
is now a mix of habitats supporting a
variety of wildlife, including great crested
newts, green and great spotted
woodpeckers, and rare burrowing bees
that make their home in the gravel banks.

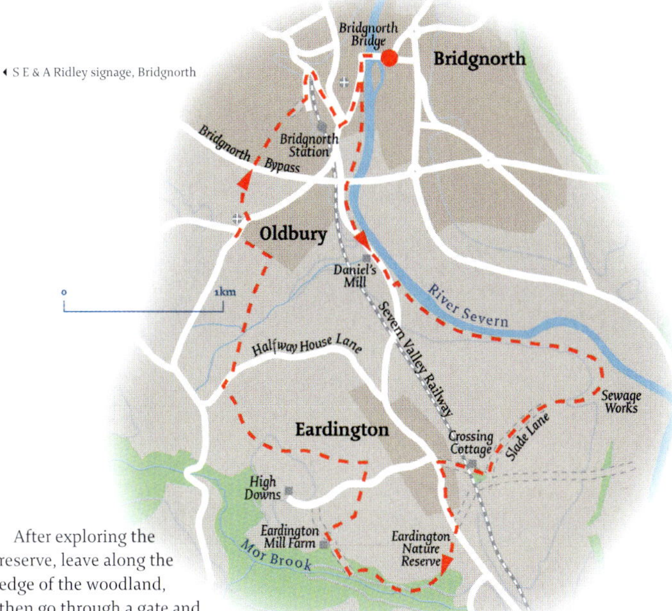

◀ S E & A Ridley signage, Bridgnorth

After exploring the reserve, leave along the edge of the woodland, then go through a gate and continue down past a couple of properties, following the marker posts through to an access lane. Follow this uphill, looking out for a gate to a path on the right soon after passing Eardington Mill Farm.

Cross the fields to emerge on a lane and cross over to enter another field. At the crossroads of paths, go left and carry on through more fields to eventually reach Halfway House Lane by the caravan and camping site. Turn right along the road and go left, following the signpost to cross a field to a footbridge.

Continue across the field to the edge of Oldbury and bear left to reach Oldbury Road. Turn right towards St Nicholas Church and take a path on the left after the church which leads to a footbridge over the bypass. Continue past the school to reach Station Lane on the other side of the tracks from Bridgnorth Station. A right turn at the end of the lane onto Hollybush Road takes you under the towering pedestrian bridge. Continue north alongside the river to return to the bridge at the start.

Hampton Loade and Dudmaston Estate

Distance 7km **Time** 2 hours 30
Terrain country roads, paths and farm
tracks **Map** OS Explorer 218
Access no public transport to the start

**Hampton Loade sits on the east bank
of the River Severn south of Bridgnorth
and for many years was connected to
Hampton on the west bank by a hand-
drawn pedestrian cable ferry. Upstream
from the site of the ferry is Dudmaston
Hall, a magnificent 17th-century country
house in the care of the National Trust.**

Leave the National Trust car park at
Hampton Loade and walk back up the hill
on the road, away from the river. Just past
the farm buildings, look for a gate into a
field and a path which soon turns right to
cross the waterworks access road and
leads to a small woodland. Cross a stream
and follow the signed path across fields to
emerge at Quatt Farm Shop on the A442.

Turn left on the road and follow the
pavement to the junction with an old
drinking well by St Andrew's Church.
Walk up through the estate village,
passing the church, and bear left on a
track which goes through an orchard.
Follow the path along the field edges to a
farm track which leads to the car park by
Dudmaston Estate's sawmill.

Turn left on the lane. Across the road is
an optional path which goes to Comer
Wood where there are several signposted
circular walking routes. Otherwise
continue down the road towards the A442
again and take care crossing over to walk
up the drive to Dudmaston Hall.

The National Trust property is a typical
Shropshire country estate with extensive
parkland, gardens and woodlands, as well
as the planned village at Quatt designed
by John Birch for the workers of the
estate. The hall also contains an art

◄ Farmland near Dudmaston Hall

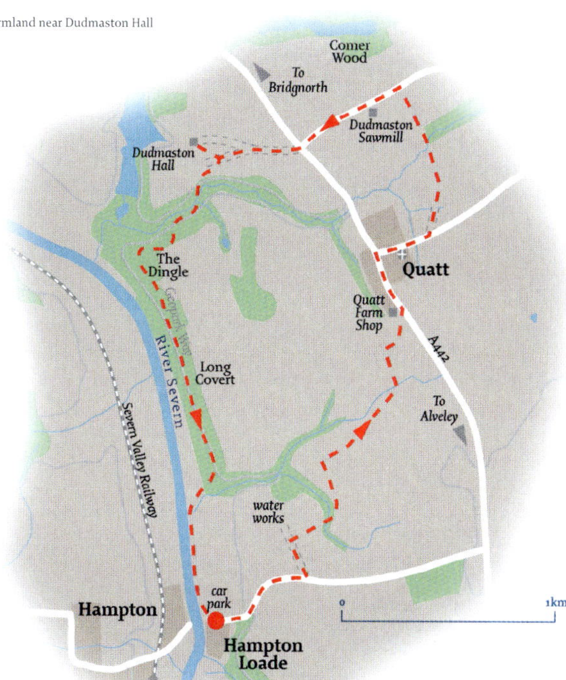

collection which includes paintings and sculptures by Henry Moore, Ben Nicholson and Barbara Hepworth, and a fine group of mid-20th-century Spanish paintings, collected by former owner Sir George Labouchere during his travels with the diplomatic service.

If not detouring to visit the house, branch left at the top of the driveway once past the car park to explore the Dingle, a romantic piece of late 19th-century landscaping on the banks of the Severn.

The Geopark Way, a 175km-long walking route from Bridgnorth to Gloucester, can be picked up at the edge of the Dingle and followed all the way back along the river to the car park at Hampton Loade.

Severn Valley Country Park

Distance 7.2km **Time** 2 hours
Terrain footpaths, pavements
Map OS Explorer 218 **Access** regular buses
to Alveley and Highley from Bridgnorth

**The beautiful Severn Valley is home to
a Green Flag Award-winning country park
with woodlands, wetlands, ponds, rivers
and wildflower meadows covering 126
acres on both sides of the river.**

Start from the Severn Valley Country
Park car park outside Alveley and follow
the path down to cross the River Severn.

The bridge here is a replacement for
what is thought to have been the world's
first concrete cantilever bridge of its kind
when it opened in 1936 to take coal and
miners across the river. At one time, more
than 1000 miners were employed in
Alveley and Highley, and when the mines
closed in 1969 the area was left derelict
and covered in spoil heaps. Since then the
land has been reclaimed, drainage ditches
dug, the spoil heaps graded and countless
trees planted.

Once over the bridge, go left through
the woods and up a steep wooden
staircase to cross over the railway tracks
when safe to do so. The Severn Valley
Railway is a heritage line which runs
steam and diesel engines between
Bridgnorth and Kidderminster.

Continue up the lane, which becomes
Barke Street, a terrace of red-brick former
miners' houses, before joining Highley's
High Street. Turn right, then quickly left
down Silverdale Terrace and just past the
allotments, go right between houses to
the playing fields. Cross the grass
diagonally to come out of the short lane
onto Redstone Drive. Follow this around
to Elizabeth Grove and go up Jubilee Drive

◄ Highley Station

before taking the path off to the left which comes out on Netherton Lane.

Turn left and follow this past Netherton House before going left just after the red postbox in the wall. Follow this path back to St Mary's Church and walk through the churchyard to a gate in the bottom corner to emerge on the High Street. Turn left and continue to Smoke Alley on the right, following this down to Station Road.

Continue down the road to the entrance of the Highley side of the Severn Valley Country Park and pick up the path that winds down to the Engine House Visitor Centre and Highley Station. The Engine House is home to out-of-service locomotives, wagons and coaches and various artefacts detailing the history of Britain's railways.

Cross the railway footbridge and follow the riverside path all the way back to the concrete bridge over the Severn that you crossed at the start of the walk.

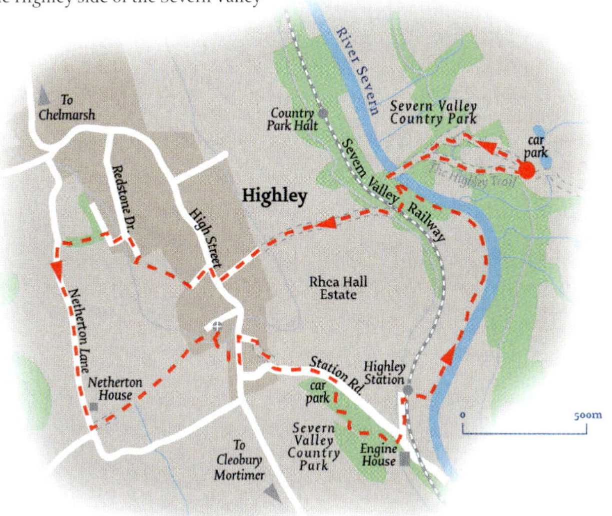

Much Wenlock and Wenlock Edge

Distance 7.75km **Time** 2 hours
Terrain footpaths and country roads
Maps OS Explorer 217 and 242
Access regular buses to Much Wenlock
from Telford

With several medieval 'black and white' buildings, a 16th-century Guildhall, the ruins of a 12th-century priory and a nature-rich limestone escarpment nearby, few towns have as much storied history and charm as Much Wenlock.

From the little clocktower in the square, head left down High Street towards the crossroads of Smithfield Road and Victoria Road. Continue along Victoria Road and veer off left to join Stretton Road just after the old Birchfield Garage. Continue on Stretton Road, following the signs for Wenlock Edge, and turn right onto the signposted lane behind houses.

This leads onto Blakeway Hollow on Wenlock Edge, following the Jack Mytton Way. As you approach the main woods, ignore the first path on the right through a gate; continue on for about 100m before bearing right along the edge of the woods.

The tree-covered limestone escarpment of Wenlock Edge was created more than 425 million years ago when this area was the floor of a tropical Silurian sea, and contains many fossils hidden in the rocks, including shells, trilobites and coral. The limestone has long been exploited for building material and burnt in small limekilns, some of which have been restored by the National Trust. The escarpment is also the ideal environment for wild garlic, bluebells, thyme, purple vetch and pyramidal orchids.

When the path emerges onto the main road at the top of Harley Hill, take care as you turn right and cross to continue on a footpath. Keep to the path as it turns left, then goes right along the edge of the woodland with views towards The

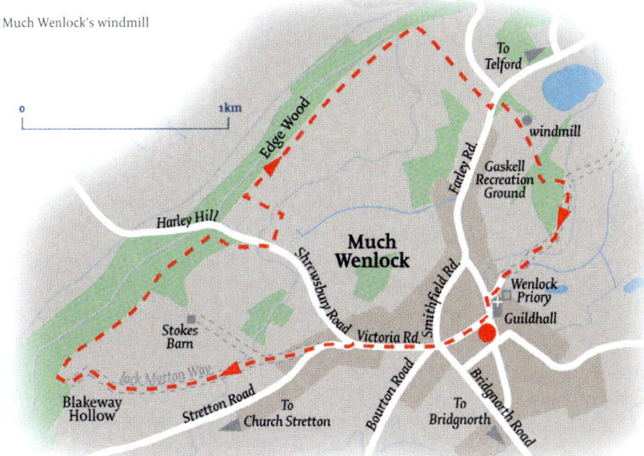

Wrekin. Carry on along the edge of the field as the path bears right to meet Farley Road, and cross over to continue back into woodland on Windmill Hill.

Much Wenlock's 17th-century windmill is on the other side of the trees and there are good views over the town from here. The path continues into the woodland behind the school and the Gaskell Recreation Ground, the rather improbable birthplace of the modern Olympic Games. In 1850, locally-born Dr William Penny Brookes had the idea to revive the Olympian ideal by staging games in his home town for people of 'every grade', which included quoit-throwing and cricket. Baron Pierre de Coubertin, the Frenchman more associated with the modern Olympic Games, was inspired to stage the first modern games in Athens in 1896 after visiting the pioneering Dr Brookes in Much Wenlock.

Bear left in the woodland to cross over the old railway track which was originally built to carry locally-quarried limestone. The signposted path soon leads to a tarmac track which winds downhill to the remains of Wenlock Priory, passing fields once farmed by the Cluniac monks.

Although the ruins date from the 12th century, an abbey was first established here in the 7th century. The original monastery, before it was destroyed by invading Danes, was the home of Milburga, a Benedictine abbess venerated as the patron saint of wild and pet birds in the Middle Ages as she was said to be able to command her feathered friends to stop eating the monastery's grain crop.

From the priory continue down the lane past Priory Hall, and turn left to pass Holy Trinity Church and the town's Guildhall before returning to the town square.

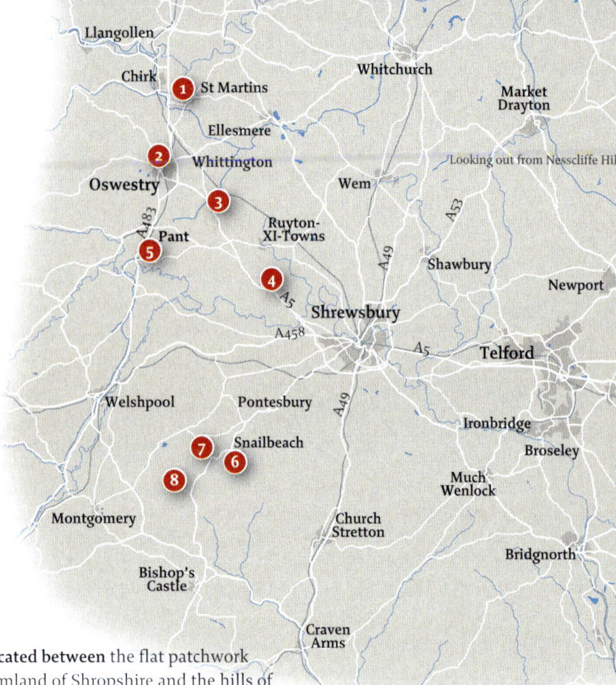

Located between the flat patchwork farmland of Shropshire and the hills of Wales, the busy market town of Oswestry has attracted drovers and traders from east and west since the Middle Ages. It has been strategically important for much longer, however, and on the northern edge of town is a remarkable Iron Age hillfort, one of the best-preserved in Britain with a great view over the border. Offa's Dyke, the ancient earthwork which delineated an early Mercian kingdom, is not far away to the west.

The Llangollen and Montgomery Canals and the Dee and Severn Rivers also make their way across the border around here, and the peaceful towpaths and riverside trails are utilised in several walks.

Further south, the tree-crowned summit of Bromlow Callow was a welcome sight for drovers taking livestock to market and the mysterious standing stones of Mitchell's Fold have long cast a spell over visitors. The Stiperstones National Nature Reserve is this area's biggest attraction, however, and the airy ridge, dotted with towering quartzite rock tors, is well-walked. The village of Snailbeach, once home to an important lead mine, is one of the quieter access points for the reserve.

West Shropshire

St Martins and Ifton Meadows

Distance 7.2km **Time** 2 hours
Terrain footpaths, country lanes and
canal towpath **Map** OS Explorer 240
Access regular buses to St Martins from
Oswestry and Ellesmere

**The land around St Martins, just north
of Oswestry, was mined for coal for more
than 400 years up to the closure of Ifton
Colliery in 1968. The spoil heaps have
been reclaimed by nature and become
a valuable wildlife habitat, as well as a
lovely place to walk.**

From St Martins' main shopping area
around Stans Superstore, start the walk by
going on past the petrol station and onto
the playing fields. Skirt around the
football pitch and exit behind the dugout
to cross a field and emerge on Clarks Lane.
Turn right and at the staggered crossroads
follow the sign along to the entrance of
Ifton Meadows Local Nature Reserve.

Ifton Colliery was the largest in
Shropshire, employing over 1300 men at
one time, and its workings crossed the
border into Wales. The site is home to
skylarks and woodpeckers, bats,
dragonflies, adders and grizzled skipper
butterflies; visitors are asked to keep dogs
on a lead, particularly during the skylark
breeding season from April to July.

There are a number of paths in the
reserve and at the entrance there are
information boards explaining the history
of the colliery. For this walk, keep to the
right-hand path, skirting the edge of the
reserve to reach a viewpoint with views
towards the Clwydian Hills. After the
viewpoint, follow the path down into a
wooded area; the path isn't too clear here
but will lead to a gate and a road.

Go left up the road and bear right as the
road bends left. Continue along to reach a
stone bridge before a steep climb to Rhyn

◄ The Ifton Colliery Memorial Statue in St Martins

Lane. Go left and follow this for just over 1km until you reach a Wat's Dyke Way stile and footpath on the left. This crosses a field to meet Nefod Lane. (If there are livestock in the field and you want to avoid this, just carry on to Nefod Lane and turn left.)

Stay on Nefod Lane past several houses to reach the B5070. Go left here and cross the bridge, then turn right shortly after, following the signposts, past a couple of houses. The path continues through trees and over the old railway embankment before meeting the Llangollen Canal at Preeshenlle Bridge.

Go left down onto the towpath and follow it past the houses of St Martin's Moor and under the road until the canal gently bends to the right.

Here, take the footpath away from the canal on the left which leads onto Church Lane in St Martins. Go right on the lane to pass St Martins Parish Church, then left to follow Green Lane back to Stans Superstore and the start.

Look out at the crossroads for the statue of a miner by local artist George Triggs which was commissioned to mark the 50th anniversary of the closure of Ifton Colliery. Plaques outlining the history of the pit and remembering the men who lost their lives working there are nearby.

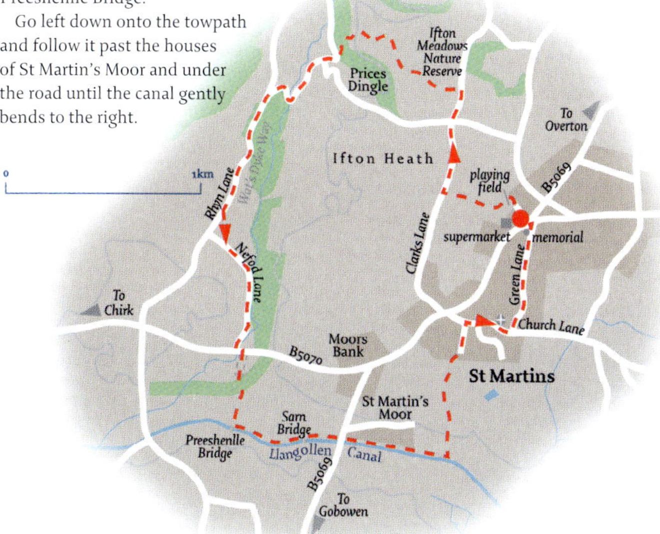

Oswestry and Old Oswestry Hillfort

Distance 6.3km **Time** 1 hour 45
Terrain pavements, footpaths and fields
Map OS Explorer 240 **Access** regular buses
to Oswestry from Shrewsbury

Occupied between 800BC and 43AD, Old Oswestry is one of the biggest and best-preserved Iron Age hillforts in England. This walk explores the multiple ramparts of this remarkable 3000-year old site, said to be the birthplace of King Arthur's Queen Guinevere, following a quick tour of the historic market town of Oswestry.

Oswestry is the third largest town in Shropshire, after Telford and Shrewsbury, and being so close to the border changed hands between the Welsh and English a number of times in the Middle Ages.

From the car park behind the town's magnificent Guildhall, head down Albion Hill and turn right on Leg Street, then go left along Oswald Road. Soon turn right along Black Gates Street and then head left just before the supermarket to go over the level crossing. To the left is the Cambrian Railways Museum, housed in the former goods depot of the Cambrian Railways Company who were headquartered in Oswestry. Next to the museum is the old station building and an original signalbox.

Once across the railway line, enter Wilfred Owen Green and aim for the grassy maze. Locally-born Wilfred Owen was the son of an employee of the railway and became the greatest war poet of the First World War. He was killed in action in November 1918, a week before the end of the war in one of the last attacks on German lines at the Sambre-Oise Canal.

Bear right at the grassy maze and go up to the trig point on Shelf Bank (145m) for more views over the town. Continue down to Queen Elizabeth Drive and follow it to Unicorn Road. Go left, then head left again on Whittington Road to pass under the old railway bridge. Turn right into Gobowen Road, then cross over into Jasmine Gardens. Continue until a path appears on the right and head up into Llwyn Coppice, then cut across the play area to the road; the hillfort is in view from here. Turn right along Llwyn Road to the car park at its foot.

There is a short climb to the top of the hillfort and then a circular loop around the top. The hillfort was abandoned by the local Cornovii or Ordovices tribes around the time of the Roman conquest and was later incorporated into Wat's Dyke, a 60km bank and ditch which divided the Anglo-Saxon kingdom of Mercia from the Welsh kingdoms to the west. At the top are views towards the Shropshire Plain, the south Shropshire hills, The Wrekin to the east and the north Welsh hills to the west. Wilfred Owen trained in trench warfare here while stationed nearby.

Return to the car park and go through the gate opposite into a field. The view back towards the hillfort gives a good sense of its size and importance. Once through the field, continue past the playing fields to Gatacre Avenue. Follow it down, taking the second left to join Liverpool Road. Go right, then left down Ash

Road and continue on Prince Street to reach Castle Street. Go right, then left down Chapel Street to the entrance to the grounds of long-gone Oswestry Castle near the start.

The site of the medieval motte and bailey is worth exploring for the views over the town; unfortunately, Oliver Cromwell's Roundheads demolished the castle in 1644 after it had been garrisoned by Royalists during the Civil War.

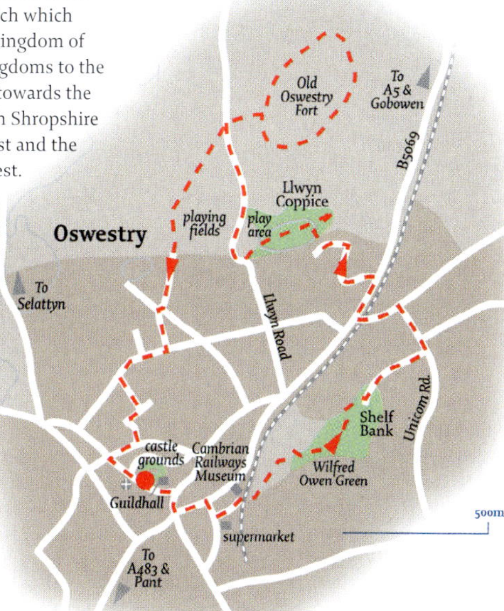

Queens Head and St Winifred's Well

Distance 11km **Time** 2 hours 45
Terrain canal towpath, fields, country
roads **Map** OS Explorer 240 **Access** regular
buses to Queens Head from Shrewsbury
and Oswestry

The Montgomery Canal – known locally
as the 'Monty' – fell into disuse in the
1940s, but this section near the hamlet
of Queens Head has been restored for
pleasure boaters. In the long period of
neglect, however, the canal and its
surroundings became home to an array of
wildlife; look out for kingfishers, grey
wagtails, damselflies and otters on the
first part of this loop which returns to the
start via country lanes.

Sharing its name with the local inn,
Queens Head is a canal hamlet situated
near the village of West Felton just off the
A5 from Oswestry and Shrewsbury. Start
the walk from the inn, cross over the canal
and take the towpath under the A5

towards the Aston Locks nature reserve
and Site of Special Scientific Interest.

At Lock No 1, you can make a short
detour around a wetland area by crossing
the lock and following a circular route
around a wooded island. Ponds like these
are home to a staggering variety of plants,
insects, birds, fish and amphibians.
Return to the lock and continue to Lock
No 2 where there is another detour
around a wild wetland site which rejoins
the canal at Lock No 3. The highlight of
this loop is the decorated main hide,
The Otter Holt, which looks out over a
large pool.

From Lock No 3, continue on the
towpath to the old inland port of
Maesbury Marsh. In the canal's heyday
this was the main commercial hub for the
area with goods arriving at wharfs and
warehouses which were built to store and
distribute milk, cheese, salt and bricks
from Cheshire, cast-iron goods from

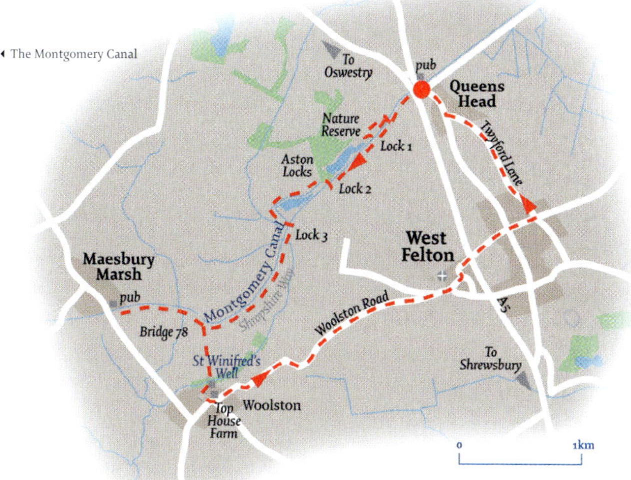

Coalbrookdale, coal from Morda, Chirk and Ruabon and limestone from the kilns of Llanymynech. The nearby Navigation Inn (the Navvy) is housed in one of the old canal-side warehouses.

From Maesbury Marsh, return to Bridge 78 and take the footpath across a field towards the hamlet of Woolston. Go over a footbridge and pass St Winifred's Well which flows out from beneath a wooden well chapel in a beautiful setting. A place of pilgrimage since the 12th century, the well is dedicated to a 7th-century Welsh princess. According to legend, she was decapitated by a spurned suitor and miraculously brought back to life by her uncle. Centuries later, her bones were laid here overnight on the way to Shrewsbury Cathedral and healing waters have sprung from the ground ever since.

Continue through the hamlet, turning left after Top House Farm to follow the quiet country road to West Felton. As you approach the village, it is worth detouring to explore the medieval motte and churchyard of St Michael's Parish Church before returning to Woolston Road. Former Prime Minister Boris Johnson married his first wife, Allegra Mostyn-Owen, here in 1987.

Follow the road to Threadneedle Street and then The Avenue, crossing the bridge over the busy A5 to reach a crossroads. Cross over and continue down School Road. At the junction with Twyford Lane, turn left to return to Queens Head.

Nesscliffe Hill and Kynaston's Cave

Distance 7.4km **Time** 2 hours
Terrain woodland paths, some single-
track road **Map** OS Explorer 240
Access regular buses to Nesscliffe from
Shrewsbury and Oswestry

In the 16th century Nesscliffe Hill
was the hideout of 'Wild' Humphrey
Kynaston, the errant son of the High
Sheriff of Shropshire, who was outlawed
by Henry VII after he murdered a man.
Today the hill is home to a popular
country park and a cave named after the
local nobleman turned brigand.

The village of Nesscliffe is found just off
the A5, midway between Oswestry and
Shrewsbury. The walk starts from the Oak
car park (free) on Hopton Lane, the end of
which is across the road from the bus stop
and the Old Three Pigeons Inn. The inn
has been serving the community since
1407 and was frequently visited by
Humphrey Kynaston and his faithful
horse, Beelzebub. The outlaw's chair is
still there, carved into the stone next to
the fireplace.

From the parking area, head into the
woods and bear left, soon looping around
and up to Oliver's Point. The way is
clearly marked and after a short climb
past the site of an old Iron Age hillfort,
which was later occupied by Roman
military, you reach a sandstone edge with
views (slightly obscured by Scots pine)
towards the Breiddens to the south and
northwest towards Oswestry. The
viewpoint is thought to be named after
Oliver Cromwell, whose Roundheads
perhaps camped here.

From the viewpoint, double back along
a section of the Shropshire Way and go
through two gates either side of a field to
reach the road. Cross over and head
towards the Pine car park, bearing left
midway through the parking area for a
pleasant detour through woodland before

rejoining the track which emerges on Valeswood Lane.

Go right on the lane, then soon turn left at a house at a crossroads onto a track signposted for The Cliffe. Follow the track and path up a wooded incline and pass rocky sandstone outcrops and a fenced-off reservoir to reach another viewpoint and The Cliffe's trig point.

Continue north through woodland for about 1km to a marker post and a water hydrant sign, then take a sharp right to begin the return to Valeswood Lane. The path back runs parallel to the outward route through heathland. After reaching Valeswood Lane, go right to meet the crossroads passed earlier and this time follow the signposted track by the community noticeboard. Pass some houses and soon pick up a path which leads back through the woodland to the Pine car park.

Carry on through the parking area and cross back over the lane to retrace your steps through the field. When you reach the trees, follow the signs left for Kynaston's Cave.

Continue through the woodland, which is dotted with sequoia trees and children's dens, then take care on the steep descent to the foot of the sandstone cliff which was home to Humphrey

Kynaston from around 1491 to 1518. The cave consists of two compartments (one for the highwayman and one for his horse) reached by a long flight of steps; there is no public access to the interior of the cave. According to local lore, the hideout was kept a secret by his supporters while Humphrey robbed from the rich who passed beneath the hill and gave to the poor in the style of the fictional Robin Hood.

Return to the Oak car park from the cave on the signposted path, enjoying views of the impressive cliffs along the way.

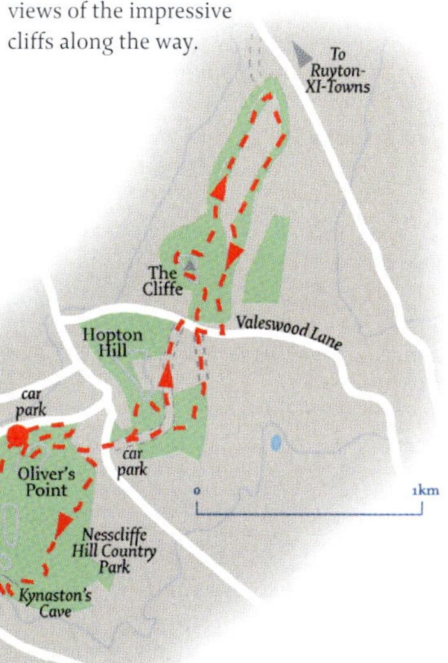

Llanymynech quarry and canal

Distance 10.45km **Time** 2 hours 30 **Terrain** footpaths, pavement, field edges and canal towpath **Map** OS Explorer 240 **Access** regular buses to Llanymynech from Shrewsbury and Oswestry

Llanymynech has been an important settlement since a hillfort was established above the present-day village in the Bronze Age. In Anglo-Saxon times Offa's Dyke went through the village on the east side of the main street. Canal, and later rail, transport allowed limestone quarrying and burning to produce quicklime, which was used by farmers to 'sweeten' their land, by ironmasters to extract iron from iron ore and by builders for mortar. This walk takes in industrial heritage and great viewpoints, following long-established paths, with an optional detour to tick off Llanymynech Hill's trig point.

Llanymynech straddles the border between Shropshire and Wales about 12km south of Oswestry. From the centre of the village, head north to cross the bridge carrying the A483 over the Montgomery Canal and turn right into the signposted Heritage Area. The old limeworks are home to a remarkably well-preserved Hoffman kiln, one of only three in the country that survive, which was in operation from 1899 to 1914. It has two tunnel vaults which are entered via 14 round-headed arches and a 42.5m-high brick chimney.

Head out of the Heritage Area and go under the A483, then take a left up an old incline plane used to bring materials down the hillside from the quarry to the limeworks. At the top of the incline take a left towards the viewpoint. Just before the viewpoint there is a gate which takes you out of Shropshire and into Wales,

the first border crossing of this walk.

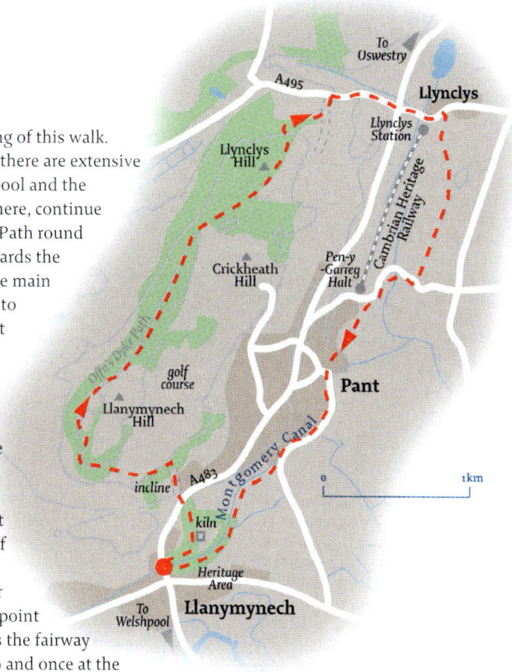

From the viewpoint there are extensive views towards Welshpool and the Breidden Hills. From here, continue along the Offa's Dyke Path round Llanymynech Hill towards the golf course. Stick to the main path here; if you want to detour to the trig point and toposcope of Llanymynech Hill (226m) wait until you reach the golf course. Once at the golf course the main path turns left; to get to the trig and toposcope go right and keep to the edge of the fairway. There is a cut-through to another fairway where the trig point comes into view. Cross the fairway when it is safe to do so and once at the trig the toposcope can be seen. Views from here are spectacular on a clear day. Retrace your steps or keep to the edge of the fairway to return to the main path.

The next section maintains height and views towards Wales as you stroll through pleasant woodland. When the Offa's Dyke Path turns off left at a crossroads keep straight on up a bank to continue towards Llynclys Hill (180m).

The path bypasses this hill and keeps going on the old Shropshire Way route to meet the A495. At the road, turn right towards the busy Llynclys crossroads. Cross the road when it is safe and follow the sign along to the Cambrian Heritage Railway at Llynclys Station.

Just after the bridge over the railway and the entrance to the station, there is a stile on the right into a field. Cross into the field and head for the stile on the other side. Follow the path and cross the stiles to go through three more fields and reach the disused Montgomery Canal. Turn right to follow the towpath all the way back to Llanymynech.

◀ The Montgomery Canal and the old limeworks chimney

Snailbeach and The Hollies

Distance 4.5km **Time** 1 hour 30
Terrain country roads, footpaths
Map OS Explorer 216 **Access** regular buses
to Snailbeach from Shrewsbury and
Bishop's Castle

The village of Snailbeach was originally
built for workers at the local lead mine,
the biggest in Shropshire and, in its
heyday, said to be the richest in Europe.
Now managed by the Shropshire Mines
Trust, the surface buildings left standing
since the mine's closure in 1955 are some
of the best preserved in the country.

The site is now a free-to-visit industrial
heritage site and a fascinating place to
spend some time. This walk explores the
area above the village, passes a peaceful
patch of rare and ancient woodland, and
accesses part of the Stiperstones National
Nature Reserve.

Snailbeach is found 3km south of
Minsterley, off the A488 Shrewsbury to
Bishop's Castle road. The walk starts from
the car park by the village hall. Directly
opposite is a signposted road and gravel
path to the site of the mine.

From the main mine site, follow the
single-track road on a fairly steep incline.
The first half of this walk is up all the way
to a height of 429m with little or no
descent till the highest point. There is
also an alternative path up through
Snailbeach Coppice which joins the road
higher up for a more natural route.

Follow the road as it bends round to the
right and Lordshill Baptist Church comes
into view. Take the road left past the
church and follow the path bearing right
alongside The Hollies, a grove of scattered
ancient holly trees, some of which are
around 400 years old. Miners working in
the nearby lead mines lived up here in
very basic cottages, keeping livestock to
supplement their earnings; holly leaves
are rich in calories and nutrients and

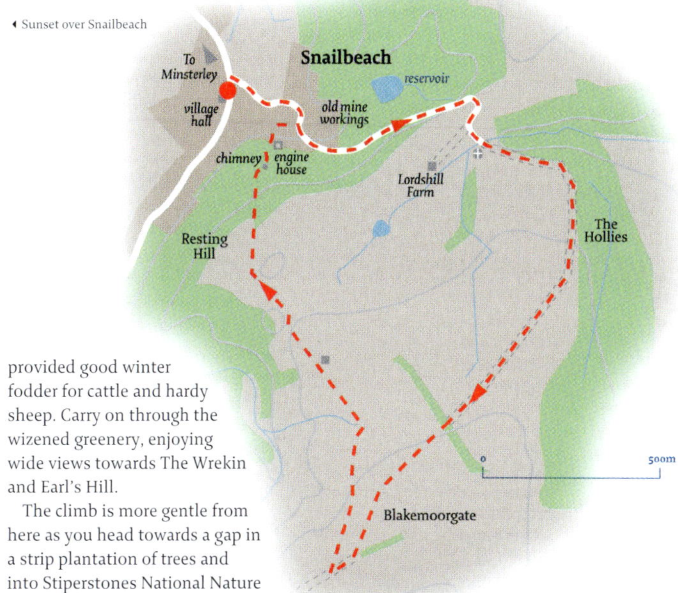

◀ Sunset over Snailbeach

provided good winter fodder for cattle and hardy sheep. Carry on through the wizened greenery, enjoying wide views towards The Wrekin and Earl's Hill.

The climb is more gentle from here as you head towards a gap in a strip plantation of trees and into Stiperstones National Nature Reserve. The Stiperstones is an outcrop of quartzite rock which rises to a height of 536m. The gradual climb soon comes to its end and a post marks the turning point after about 210m of steady ascent. The walk could easily be extended from here, however, to explore some of the notable features of the famous Stiperstones ridge, such as the Paddock, Shepherd's Rock, the Devil's Chair and Manstone Rock.

On the descent back to Snailbeach there are views towards the Welsh mountains and Corndon Hill just over the border in Wales. The path down is fairly straightforward and clings to the high side of the hill. Bear left after the gate by the high point and head through a field towards the old smelter chimney sticking out through the woodland canopy.

The path carries on through the trees to the main area of the mine workings, passing a rare surviving Cornish engine house on the way. Rejoin the access road after exploring the other mine buildings to go back down to the village hall.

Bromlow Callow

Distance 7.4km **Time** 2 hours 15
Terrain fields, paths, country roads,
farm track **Map** OS Explorer 216
Access regular buses to Hope from
Shrewsbury and Bishop's Castle

**Bromlow Callow is a distinctive hill on
the Shropshire skyline which can be seen
from miles around. Topped with hardy
Scots Pine, the iconic Callow has been a
navigational landmark for cattle drovers
on the way to market for hundreds of
years. This walk goes through several
fields which may have livestock in them,
so please keep dogs on a lead.**

The walk starts from the car park at
Hope Village Hall in the Hope Valley
which lies south of Minsterley, off the
A488 Shrewsbury to Bishop's Castle road.

From the hall, head down the road,
looking out for a stile in the hedgerow to
your left as the road goes round a bend.
Cross over and follow the path along the
field edges to emerge back onto a minor
road (Drury Lane) near the Stables Inn, an
old drovers' watering hole which was
established in 1680 to serve farmers
walking livestock to Shrewsbury Market.

Cross the road and keep right as you
traverse the farmland, heading towards
the large mansion house (Leigh Manor).
There are signposts to follow which are
reasonably visible. Soon after entering
another field, bear left and pass a pond
before heading gently up into the woods.

Once through the trees, continue
towards the road, then bear left to go back
into woodland. Emerging from the trees
again, skirt round a field to reach
Lordstone Lane. Continue up the lane for
a short distance to a signposted junction
and go downhill past some houses.

Head over the stile before the end of the
track and go through the field to another
stile. Cross a driveway and over another
stile to emerge on a lane leading to some
houses. Bear left up the lane to reach a
junction and go right, sharply downhill,
with the distinctive wooded top of
Bromlow Callow directly ahead.

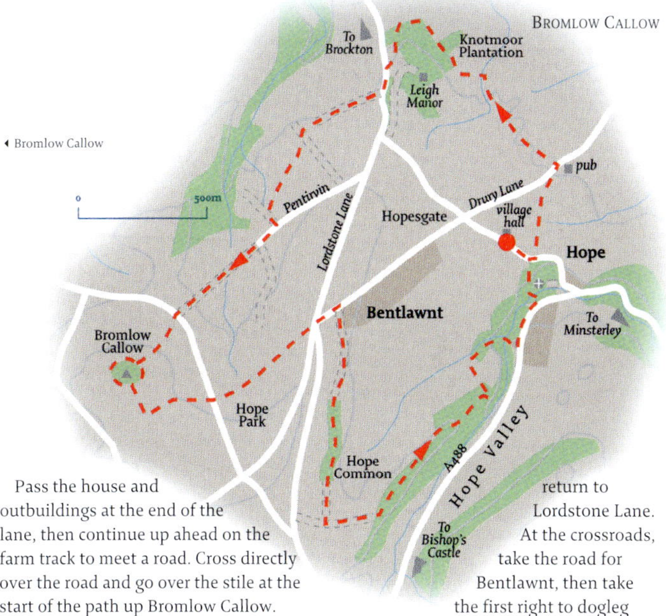

Pass the house and outbuildings at the end of the lane, then continue up ahead on the farm track to meet a road. Cross directly over the road and go over the stile at the start of the path up Bromlow Callow.

The path up the fairly short and steep incline to the top is easy to follow. Once at the top, there is the choice to either circle the summit to enjoy the views south to Stapeley Hill and Corndon Hill, to the Stiperstones ridge to the east and Shrewsbury to the north, or to head directly through the trees.

To leave the summit, take the path on the east side, aiming for the trig point on the neighbouring unnamed hill. About halfway to the trig in the dip is a marker post; go left here and follow the path back down to the road.

Cross over the road and go through the gate opposite, then follow a path through the field and several gates to return to Lordstone Lane. At the crossroads, take the road for Bentlawnt, then take the first right to dogleg down a bridleway. Follow it to the end, then continue on the path and bear left when you reach the end of Swain's Lane. Go past a few houses and through a gate towards the woodland.

Follow the densely wooded ridge to the end where the path bears left across a field towards a small brook. Follow the brook down to reach the A488, then take care heading left along the road's grassy verge for a short distance. Look out for a gate in the churchyard wall – Hope Church is concealed by trees and not visible from the road. Go through the churchyard to emerge from the hedgerow onto the lane and turn left to return to Hope Village Hall.

Mitchell's Fold

Distance 5km **Time** 1 hour 30
Terrain farm track and grassy footpaths
with steep sections **Map** OS Explorer 216
Access regular buses from Shrewsbury and
Bishop's Castle to the A488 by White Grit,
1.5km from the start

Shropshire's best-known stone circle,
Mitchell's Fold, is an enigmatic Bronze
Age stone circle constructed over 3000
years ago on the heathland at the
southwest end of Stapeley Hill (405m),
near the county's border with Wales.
The short walk from this Scheduled
Ancient Monument up to the summit of
the hill takes in sweeping views across the
Welsh mountains and the Shropshire
hills. Livestock may be grazing in the area,
so please keep dogs on a lead.

The walk begins on the very edge of
Shropshire on the road between
Priest Weston and the scattered village
of White Grit, just over the border in
Wales. There is limited roadside parking
at the end of the signposted track up to
the stone circle and another small parking
area at the dead end of the track closer
to the stones.

The stone circle is soon reached around
300m from the end of the access track.
Bronze-age settlers raised the ceremonial
circle with stones from Stapeley Hill some
time between 2000BC and 1400BC. It's
around 27m in diameter with 15 of the
original 30 or so stones still in place.
Although the stones are not as grand as
those at Stonehenge – the tallest are only
shoulder height – they do not attract
coaches and crowds, so there is more
scope for quiet contemplation.

Like many such sites, legends abound,
and Mitchell's Fold is no different. The
best known tale is that during a time of
famine, a fairy gave a magic cow to locals

◄ Standing stones of Mitchell's Fold

which provided an endless supply of milk. One night an evil witch milked the animal into a sieve and when the cow realised the cunning trick, the witch was petrified and a circle of stones was erected around her to ensure that she could never escape.

Another fanciful story has it that King Arthur drew the mythical sword of Excalibur (known as *Caledfwlch* in Welsh legend) from one of the stones here to become King of the Britons.

Behind you, over the border in Wales, is Corndon Hill (513m), which has several large Bronze Age cairns on the summit – most likely related in some way to the standing stones.

The onward path to the summit of Stapeley Hill is straightforward and goes just past the top, then climbs gently

back round to reach the cairn. Views from here take in the distinctive wooded top of Bromlow Callow to the north and the quartzite rocky outcrop of Stiperstones to the east, as well as hulking Corndon Hill to the south.

From the top of Stapeley Hill the path follows the saddle south past another cairn of an unnamed top. Keep straight on in the direction of Corndon Hill and at the end of the saddle go down a fairly steep decline to a farm track. Bear right and follow it to pass farm buildings as the track rises back up to Mitchell's Fold and the start of the walk.

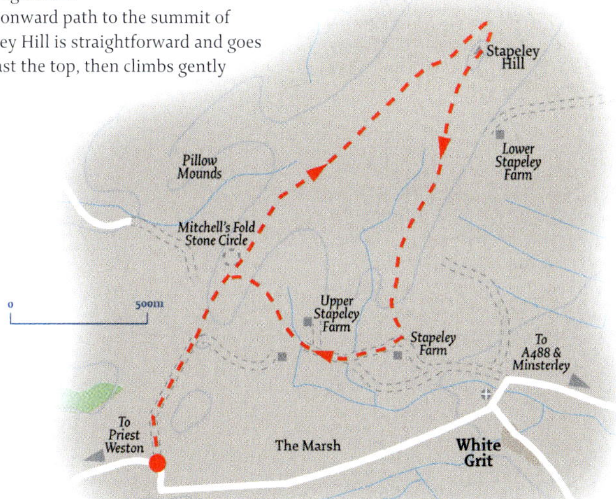

Index